SURVIVING:
When Someone You Love Was Murdered.

SURVIVING:

When Someone You Love Was Murdered.

A Professional's Guide To Group Grief Therapy For Families & Friends of Murder Victims

by
Lula M. Redmond, R.N., M.S.

Photo: Memorial Wall — HSGP

August 1989
Editor: Gary Bond, Ed.D.
Editorial Assistance: Charles Corr, Ph. D.
Photography: David Wells
Advertising Copy: Eric Gerard
Type Set: Paul McCoy, Roberts Printing, Inc.
Printing: Precision Litho Service, Inc.

Psychological Consultation and Education Services, Inc.
P.O. Box 6111, Clearwater, Florida 34618-6111

Library of Congress Catalog Card Number: 89-63404

ISBN 0-9624592-0-8

With tribute

to those who have died,

those who have survived,

and to my family with the prayer
that we may *never* know this experience.

Partial proceeds from the sale of this book will be donated to the work of the Homicide Survivors Group, Inc. of Pinellas County, Clearwater, Florida.

Foreword
by Therese A. Rando, Ph.D.
Warwick, Rhode Island
September 25, 1989

I got my first inkling about my resistance when I found myself dusting off the original manuscript I had received to review in preparation for the writing of this foreword. It had been placed in a far corner of my study — in a spot where it readily could be seen to give me the visual cues to remind me to do it, but in a place, I later realized, to be sufficiently far enough away from my other work so as not to "contaminate" it. I remember wondering why it was taking me so long to get to this project.

Several months later, in providing supervision to a therapist working with a woman whose husband had been brutally murdered by being beaten and kicked to death by a gang of teenagers, it started to dawn on me: I was trying to distance myself from the horrific aspects of murder. Although I genuinely wanted to support Lu Redmond's critically important efforts to put forth a treatment program for survivors of homicide, and having myself worked with a number of survivors, I was attempting to protect myself from the assault I knew I would experience when I read the vivid case examples illustrating her book. When I finally did get into the book, combined with my shock at reading the statistics (most notably that the probability exists for one out of every 153 persons to be murdered, and that the population of bereaved homicide survivors is 210-300,000 in one year — a significantly understated number since it includes only members in the family and not affected others outside the family system), I was stripped, as I knew I would be, of the illusion of protectiveness and control with which so many of us delude ourselves. Is it any wonder why I resisted reading the book? Yet, is it any wonder why I needed to read it?

The notion that someone intentionally can intrude into my life, cause pain to one I hold dear, rob that person of their life and me of them, and that in many cases there is absolutely nothing I can do to prevent or control it — this is powerlessness, vulnerability, and anxiety at its height. Often we try to comfort ourselves by "blaming the victim" and assuring ourselves that the one who was murdered either "deserved" it or was "asking for it" by virtue of what they were doing, where they were doing it, or with whom they were associating. However, often these attempts at self-protection fail, and we are left with the mind-boggling reality that we and our loved ones can be minding our own business, in places where we legitimately should be, surrounded by people we ought to be with, and still murder can reach out and shatter our lives forever.

The mental health professional is no less immune from the wish to recoil from these thoughts or defend against this anxiety than any layperson. Nevertheless, this professional, by virtue of the work he/she undertakes with homicide survivors, either those touched intimately or peripherally, has a moral and ethical obligation to address these issues sufficiently so that they do not end up contributing to the "secondary victimization" experienced by so many of those whose loved ones have been murdered. This is not to say that professionals should not, or indeed even could _not_ have emotional reactions to the experiences and responses to these patients/clients. Rather, it is to note that these reactions must be identified and addressed in such a fashion as to eliminate iatrogenic problems, facilitate appropriate empathy, assist in an appreciation of the survivor's predicament and, ideally, aid in the caregiver's construction of a more meaningful and appropriately prioritized personal life in recognition of the constant possibility of losing one of their own loved ones to murder.

One of the major problems in providing mental health services to various populations of mourners is that caregivers traditionally have overutilized models and schemata in an effort both to understand these populations and to make them less anxiety-provoking to themselves. Unfortunately, this has led to two distinct problems: First, mourners are lumped into specific categories of loss wherein the individual aspects of their situations and responses are overlooked (e.g., "bereaved parents," "suicide survivors," "widows," and so forth) and second, caregivers mistakenly assume that while the content of the mourning process may be different in terms of who has been lost, the experience of the mourning process always remains the same (e.g., the mourning of one who loses a child is the same as one who loses a spouse.)

While such categorizations and the erroneous actions and assumptions they give rise to are practiced by many caregivers as valid, they are not. Recent commentary on the field of thanatology argues for the necessity of discriminating among losses more carefully, recognizing the powerful impacts of the idiosyncratic factors surrounding a particular loss experience, and identifying new theoretical models and treatment interventions to respond to the fact that different losses generate different mourning experiences and mandate different treatment interventions (Rando, 1986). All griefs are not the same and cannot be treated so.

Twenty-nine separate sets of variables have been identified to influence an individual's grief response (Rando, 1984). These are grouped under the three categories of (1) psychological factors, including the characteristics and meaning of the lost relationship, the mourner's personal characteristics, and the specific circumstances of the death; (2) social factors; and (3) physical factors. Any person's response to a given death is determined by the unique constellation of factors pertinent to their particular loss. It is only after analyzing these factors that the caregiver is in a position to understand, evaluate, and, if appropriate, intervene in the mourner's responses.

In homicide, irrespective of the characteristics of either the relationship or the mourner (included under number one, psychological factors, above), the characteristics of the death are so traumatic that they can overwhelm other usually helpful assets the mourner normally would bring to bear upon dealing with a loss of a different type. Further, the severity of the trauma is known to adversely affect both the social and physical dimensions (numbers two and three above) influencing an individual's grief response. Although how all of these are experienced will be moderated by the personal characteristics of the mourner and the nature and meaning of who and what has been lost (included under number one, psychological factors, above), it is imperative to recognize the distinct issues presented in homicide and then to comprehend how they are experienced idiosyncratically by each individual mourner depending upon the constellation of factors present. It is the unique accumulation of these factors which together will comprise the fabric of the bereavement experience caregivers seek to address.

By virtue of the fact that in most cases this is a sudden death (or at least follows a sudden attack even if the victim's death does not occur immediately), the survivor is forced to experience the unanticipated grief response, known to seriously complicate recovery through its severe assault on the mourner's adaptive capacities (Parkes & Weiss, 1983). While whether a death is sudden or anticipated influences *how* the survivor will cope, the precise cause of death will influence *what* the individual must contend with, given the way the death occurred (Rando, 1988). In homicide there is an accumulation of issues which complicate the grief and mourning process and make healthy accommodation of the loss extremely difficult, although not impossible.

It is to Lu Redmond's credit that she has recognized the importance of integrating both the uniqueness of the mourner, his/her loss, and the personal experience, with the commonalities of the homicide bereavement experience. With regard to the latter, she presents abundant clinical information while outlining a 12 session group therapy format, thus capitalizing on the treatment of choice for traumatized victims while recognizing both economic and staff constraints. She addresses the issues arising out of preventability (this death did not *have to happen),* and engendering the critical topic of blame and responsibility, noting that the survivor must cope with anger at the responsible agent, probably spending great time and effort looking for the reason, attempting to find some meaning, and striving to regain some sense of control. She delineates how the violent and traumatic nature of a homicide increases helplessness and threat, and exacerbates fear, vulnerability, and feeling out of control. In itself, she writes, this not only complicates mourning and subsequent adaptation, but also often interferes with the appropriate receipt of social support from others, leading to additional perceptions of injustice and unfairness. She assists the reader in comprehending why, in the absence of a specific agent for blame, when the perpetrator is not identified and caught, all of these feelings not only can be exacerbated, but, additionally, can be worsened when survivors blame themselves in some fashion because they find it easier to deal with a traumatic event being their responsibility (and thus within their control), than to cope with the fact that it was a truly random event over which no one had any control. It is a high price, but one they unconsciously pay to maintain a sense that the world is not so arbitrary and so unpredictable, thereby minimizing the fright associated with the recognition we cannot protect ourselves against truly random events.

Offering additional psychological insight into survivors, Ms. Redmond describes how, if the murderer was someone the loved one knew, anger and distress that the victim was involved with that person can permeate the bereaved's response, along with guilt for not having intervened in the relationship, especially if it is believed one could have done something to prevent the murder. Tying guilt in this situation in with what is evidenced after other losses, she describes how guilt also may be experienced for what one did or didn't do that put the victim at the scene of the murder, in addition to all the typical reasons for guilt known to exist after any major loss.

Looking at how this type of loss sustains a particularly heavy burden of inherent negative factors which must be understood in their context by caregivers who are unafraid to reach out to those reacting intensely, Ms. Redmond illuminates for us that in homicide no death is acceptable, no death is timely, no death is anticipated, no death is unpreventable, no death surround is comforting. Each of these potentially ameliorating factors is missing in this type of loss. Further, no matter what rationale the murderer may have had, to the survivor it is a senseless and unnecessary event. Rage at the violence, helplessness, and lack of control in the face of it, is incredible and the survivor will require time and support in learning how to channel it in order that it not become personally destructive to him/her. The normal fear elicited in most situations of acute grief, wherein the mourner is frightened by the depth and intensity of heretofore seldom experienced volatile emotions, can reach its zenith after experiencing the murder of a loved one. Desires for revenge and retribution must be normalized, yet eventually must be focused constructively so as not to bring additional loss and devastation. The caregiver will require proper information, strength and conviction, and support to tolerate these hostile affects and assist in their appropriate working through and the ultimate empowerment of the survivor. The necessary resources, strategies, and rationales for achieving this are discussed in the ensuing chapters.

One of the preventable, but all too frequently inevitable, tragedies of surviving a loved one's homicide is the mourner having to experience a lack of social responses that contribute to "secondary victimization." Systems existing to assist survivors prepetuate this type of occurrence and add insult to injury by violating and frustrating the needs and expectations of the survivor victims who turn to them. Parties guilty of such abuse include other family and friends, the law enforcement and criminal justice systems, the media, mental health and human service professionals, educators, and the clergy, among others. As Ms. Redmond sadly notes, in instances where there is less secondary victimization these survivors had less complicated bereavement reactions considering other factors. The implications for what the "system" does for survivors, by burdening them when they already are overwhelmingly overburdened, are unconscionable and Ms. Redmond delineates the necessary strategies to minimize it if it must occur at all. She additionally discusses the major problem of mourners who intentionally must repress their grief and mourning during legal investigation and court proceedings. The fact that this repression is intentional does not minimize its impact upon the survivor, who suffers the same effects of repression as does any mourner who fails to engage in the requisite processes of grief and mourning. It is another unique onus placed upon those already oppressed by tragedy, pain, confusion, lack of meaning and rage. For some it must be borne for many years after their loved one has been taken from them, as legal proceedings can drag on for years and the consequences of intentional repression often do not disappear without leaving many scars and much disruption.

For those who have the courage to work with life's most victimized individuals, this book provides a veritable compendium of riches. Poignantly illustrated with relevant and instructive case examples from Ms. Redmond's extensive experience, the book compiles all the information that any caregiver could desire: theoretical (e.g., "What is the adaptive purpose of the rage?"), clinical (e.g., "Do not make the mistake of putting a survivor in a homicide group too early."), practical (e.g., "What do you do about getting information about cleaning up the blood after a murder?"), and organizational (e.g., reading resources and homework assignments for group members and therapists). Her step-by-step group therapy for survivors and her training for mental health professionals gradually empowers both groups as they each struggle to confront the myriad issues posed by homicide. The "lessons" she presents which she has been taught by homicide survivors provide substantive and previously lacking clinical data about what works, what doesn't, and why. For those desiring to start a similar group, the legwork has all been done and is offered here for immediate use, from sample letters of inquiry for solicitation of funds to sample intake and release forms, from therapist study questions to homework for dealing with ambivalence and unfinished business, from creation of a memorial service ritual to a screening intake format for choosing group members.

Ms. Redmond has avoided all the pitfalls encountered by many of the current authors in clinical thanatology. She has kept an individualistic perspective, yet not forgotten to examine the commonalities that are shared in this type of loss. She has addressed treatment, but has not short-changed assessment. She has focused on survivor victims and the provision of services to them, but has integrated this with the ongoing training of mental health professionals. She has provided an excellent theoretical review of all multidisciplinary literature, while distilling the clinically practical information for intervention. She has confronted caregivers on their resistance to working with homicide survivors, while simultaneously providing us with the information, insight, and tools to remedy this serious omission.

In conclusion, it is safe to say that there can be no question that homicide predisposes survivors to more complicated mourning and poorer bereavement outcomes. It is a type of loss which terrifies both the victims and those who observe them. Yet despite this, people *can* and *do* survive the murder of a loved one, although not without extraordinary pain, anguish, and other significant psychosocial, spiritual, physical, and economic distress. For those who care, the challenge is how to help minimize the distress for the survivors, so that it is not worse than it has to be, and to maximize the conditions for healthy empowerment and integration of this tragedy into their lives. Lu Redmond has given us some priceless guidelines on how to do both.

Bibliography

Parkes, C. & Weiss, R. *Recovery from bereavement*. New York: Basic Books, 1983.

Rando, T.A. *Grief, dying, and death: Clinical interventions for caregivers*. Champaign, IL: Research Press, 1984.

Rando, T.A. Introduction. In T.A. Rando (Ed.), *Parental loss of a child*. Champaign, IL: Research Press, 1986, xi-xiv.

Rando, T.A. *Grieving: How to go on living when someone you love dies*. Lexington, MA: Lexington Books, 1988.

ACKNOWLEDGEMENTS

There are four categories of persons who have made the writing and publishing of this book possible. First, there are those who supported and encouraged my education and experience in the fields of thanatology and victimology.

Secondly, there are the colleagues who were willing to critically critique the organization and design of a treatment program, the first co-leaders and victim advocates, who willingly risk putting an idea into practice, and assisted with the formation.

Thirdly, there are the survivors who have been our teachers without whom we would not have learned how best to meet their needs. And, the survivors in the pilot project who resolved to help all those who followed in their footsteps.

And fourth, there are my colleagues, family and friends who have encouraged this project to be shared, who reviewed early editions and offered suggestions, and assisted in the many tasks of the production of a book.

My father, Christopher John Moshoures, encouraged my education. He believed you could do anything if you had an education. He expected me to become a physician. I knew that,and resisted with all my being. I became a nurse instead. I later took my first family therapy course in graduate school and knew I had to become a family therapist. In some ways I had been a family therapist, prior to knowledge of the theories, most of my life. I believe in the strength of the family and the power within the family to heal itself.

After graduate school, I was fortunate to study at Georgetown University Family Center, in Washington, D.C., under Dr. Murray Bowen It was the study of Bowen Family Systems that sparked my drive to learn more and become a private practitioner of Family Therapy. I am forever grateful to the teaching and learning process that Dr. Bowen imparted. The concepts of his theory made sense and I have had the experience of seeing family after family become functional and emotionally stronger once again. I see my position of therapist as a coach and educator. The strategy, plays, and moves may be directed by the coach but it is the family team members who play to win the game.

I knew that death was one of the most severe crises a family must endure so began the study of Thanatology. I felt if I could wed the literature, research, theories, and experiences of death education and family therapy, that I may have something to offer suffering families to help them become whole again. I became a clinical thanatologist, family therapist with a specialty in grief therapy. My status as a healer would have satisfied my father had he lived. He was a healer who did not have the opportunity of a formal education. This has been my life's work since my husband's death in 1974. Prior to that I was a Navy wife for 25 years. I am forever a mother and a grandmother.

It has been the process of learning for which I am most grateful. I have been so fortunate in my personal life. Many survivors ask if I am a homicide survivor. I am thankful that no one in my family has been murdered. When I was eight years old the girl who was employed by my family to care for my brothers and me was murdered in the bedroom which she and I shared. It is an early vivid memory. I have greater understanding of that experience now. I loved Pauline. She was my friend.

I have experienced deep painful grief. Five members of my family, including my father and husband, died in a four year period. These experiences made me aware of the need for greater knowledge. I also recognized the need to do my own ''grief work'' prior to working with grieving clients. I was able to do that with the help of Mary Waterman, to whom I shall always be grateful. In 1976 I was fortunate to meet Dr. Dan Leviton of the University of Maryland. He had just formed the Forum For Death Education and Counseling, Inc. which has been renamed the Association for Death Education and Counseling, Inc. (ADEC). Dan instills confidence with conviction and I am grateful for his encouragements. He *knows* you can be more than you thought you could ever be. In 1979 he gave me the opportunity to teach about death in family systems in national workshops, when it was still a concept unexplored by many therapists.

I am indebted to my colleagues and friends, Dana Cable, Charles Corr, Alice Demi, Helen Fitzgerald, Jeanne Harper, Gene Knott, Terry Martin, Joan McNeil, Marge Miles, Terri Rando, Edie Stark, John Stephenson, Hannelore Wass, and Ellen Zinner among many others. I had the opportunity to attend their presentations throughout the years at the ADEC conferences. With some I served as a co-faculty member. Each one has added depth to my thinking. I appreciate the teachings of Dr. William Worden and have used his work extensively for many years as well as throughout this book.

My study of victimology has been inspired by both Dr. Marlene Young of the National Organization for Victim Assistance in Washington, D.C., and the work of the National Victim Center in Fort Worth, Texas. I was honored by the invitation to write the modules on *Crisis Intervention* and the *Mental Health Needs of Victims* for the National Victim Center's Conference Manual. That task spurred my interest to complete this manuscript. The needs are so great and the references so limited in the field at this time.

Eight years ago when I experienced working with my first family of homicide survivors, this book began to take shape in my imagination. I knew I was seeing trauma unlike any that I had heard of in my graduate studies, family therapy courses, or in seminars and conferences.

I avoided taking families of homicide victims for the first three years in my private practice as a grief therapist. I was certain there were experts in the field who were more knowledgeable and hence could be more therapeutic than I. It was the first case that I accepted that made me know that I must learn about this population of forgotten mourners. I personally telephoned every mental health agency in the area to try to secure assistance for the family whose 14 year old had been murdered. There was not any assistance, there was not even any referral sources, there were rebuttals. I explained my lack of knowledge and experience to the family and my services were still requested. I accepted the case to learn, as much as to assist. I learned. To my amazement the family grew in two years to be totally productive, functional and strong again. I knew my coaching had a part in that growth. I was challenged!

Within months of the first case, the victim advocate of the Pinellas County Sheriff's Department, Sara Sopkin Prugh, began talking of the need for an organized program. Ms. Prugh had left the area to attend law school by the time we began working on the program design. Her colleagues, Kathy Corr and Laura White, victim advocates, took an active interest and worked diligently for over a year before we were able to organize the pilot program.

The work, persuasion, support, concern and compassion of these two professionals made the program possible. I thank each of them for myself and all the survivors of homicide who have benefited from those early years of work.

I am indebted to those who have willingly served as group co- leaders. It is difficult to serve in the role of student after years of serving as qualified professional therapists. It was imperative that we were willing to learn from survivors and not carry our preconceived ideas of the psychological trauma into their lives. This requires an openness, recognition that the material was new to each of us, and willingness to be flexible, changing any part of the program when required. I thank Tom Lewis, and Millie Williams from the Mental Health Services of Upper Pinellas, Inc. and their agency for support of the program. Therapists from Pinellas Emergency Mental Health Services, Inc., Pat Settle, Pattie Hearndon, Don Gates, and the support received from their agency. And appreciation to the individuals in private practice who while working within an agency gave up their personal time, effort and energy to share in this learning experience, Charles Larsen, Marvin Kassed, and Laurice Jennings. Each one has worked hard and added to our learning.

My deepest appreciation goes to the survivors of homicide who came, trusting us to do no harm, believing we could help, and who shared their personal tragedies beyond our imagination. It would be impossible to name them all. There were 62 left on the waiting list after we formed the pilot group. There are hundreds more in the years since. They are our teachers. They have been willing to share with the readers in the hope that others whose lives have been shattered may receive help. They have been willing to go out and work for funding so that our doors may remain open to all who come after them.

There are also those who *cannot* come for help. I believe we have an obligation to try to reach them and support them through their personal battles for survival. Several readers have suggested that the title of this book be changed to better reflect the content on the design of the program. A subsequent book has been planned to be titled *Surviving: When Someone You Love Was Murdered; A Layperson's Guide to Working Through Your Grief.* This will be intended for those who cannot find assistance in their community or who resist attending therapy.

I appreciate the work of my editor, Dr. Gary Bond. His insights, discussions and comments have made this a better book. The editorial work by Dr. Charles Corr and Dr. John Stephenson have increased its value to the thanatological community. I am honored by the content in the Foreword written by Dr. Therese Rando. Dr. Rando is one of the most respected authors in the field of thanatology. Her vision is great, her sense of compassion knows no bounds. I appreciate all who have given of their time, energy and expertise in reading the early manuscript of this work and who willingly offered suggestions to help make it more useful for the reader; Dr. Marlene Young of the National Organization of Victim Assistance, Janice Harris Lord of Mothers Against Drunk Driving, Pat Simpson of Parents of Murdered Children, Dr. Charles Corr of Southern Illinois University, Dr. John Stephenson in private practice in Maine, and Charles Larsen, Clinical Director of Social Services at Medfield Center in Clearwater. My deepest appreciation goes to Patricia C. Murphy and Timothy Curtiss who as survivors of homicide were members of a Group Grief Therapy Treatment Program and willingly read the manuscript risking a reawakening of fresh psychic pain. The comments of each were invaluable.

I thank Lisa Bosserman Cole, Susan Clark, Debbie Hudson and Patricia Murphy for their typing, proofreading and indexing. Their patience and diligence was extraordinary. My work with the Type Manager, Paul McCoy of Roberts Printing has been gratifying. Mr. McCoy took a personal interest in the content that far surpassed the tasks of production. My early work with Randy Reno of Precision Litho Service, Inc. has assured me of the finest quality.

There is an abundance of love and appreciation to my children and family for their encouragement and support. They have respected my need to work long hours, be the best I can be, and have loved me anyway. They are and will always be, my best friends.

TABLE OF CONTENTS

Foreword by *THERESE A. RANDO, Ph.D.*

Acknowledgments

CHAPTER ONE

CHAPTER TWO

CHAPTER THREE

CHAPTER FOUR

CHAPTER FIVE

CHAPTER SIX

APPENDIX I

APPENDIX II

"It is the victim and those who loved him who
serve a LIFE SENTENCE."

CHAPTER ONE

Introduction

The voice on the phone was frantic. You could hear the fear and sense of terror as she begged for help. The man who murdered her brother had just been released after serving a four-year sentence providing janitorial services in the local courthouse as *punishment* for his crime. Her 50-year-old brother had been killed in his home in Georgia. His neighbor had used a hacksaw to cut up his body in less than six inch pieces. The absence of gossip in this small rural town led the murderer to realize his criminal action was undiscovered. After church services he led his Sunday School class over to the victim's home. The victim's mother became blind at news of her youngest child's murder, she continues to *hear* her son, and *knows* he will come to get her soon. Subsequent eye examinations revealed no physical cause for blindness. The family has just received word that the killer who is now released may be heading south. They live in fear that he may return to kill again.

The above case is true and characterizes the life sentence served by those who become survivors of homicide. The psychological trauma of murder of a loved one leaves survivors victimized physically, emotionally, financially, socially and spiritually. No one can be prepared for the level of emotional turbulence created by murder. The survivor must grieve not only for the way a loved one died but for the loss of the person.

The work of providing psychological treatment makes it possible for survivors to continue a functional life. This book has been written to assist mental health practitioners who desire to expand practice in the field of thanatology and victimology. The use of group grief therapy is a method by which practitioners can assist those who have been victimized by murder of their loved one. For this information to be useful the therapist or counselor must be versed in basic death education. It would only be appropriate to begin a Grief Therapy Treatment Program for survivors of homicide following the study of the bereavement process in other types of deaths.

Also, it is suggested that the study must be more than the knowledge of Kubler-Ross's five stages of coping with the dying process, which to many has become a nationally accepted model. Dr. Kubler-Ross has made a tremendous contribution in her work with the dying and grieving. She was one of the first researchers "heard" by captivating the audience of nurses and medical professionals who identified with the needs of dying patients. However, a more indepth study of thanatology reveals psychodynamics about which the professional must be fully aware.

Throughout this text, materials from many leading physicians, family therapists, psychologists, mental health professionals and thanatologists will be used in reference. It is important for the reader to review the originals of the referenced studies. This text simply offers a small segment in a vast field of important and useful information to the serious and responsible therapist. Do not proceed without knowledge of the subject matter. This text may be useful to assist in serving those who suffer from other types of traumatic loss, such as rape, child and spouse abuse, or deaths from suicide or vehicular homicide. The principles are similar in working with all victims of psychological trauma.

This volume is the result of study and treatment of homicide survivors since 1982. In this work, I have been privileged to learn from many survivors of traumatic deaths. All of the stories in the case illustrations are real. The names and identifying data have been disguised to protect the anonymity of those who have shared their life story. In some cases, two or more stories with similar dynamics but different circumstances and details are used to illustrate techniques useful in treatment. I am indebted to those who have allowed their stories to be shared with the reader so that we may all learn to meet an unfulfilled need in our society. The survivors have taught that there is a better way to meet their emotional needs. This book is a personal effort toward achieving a more humane way to care for the thousands who have been bereaved by the hand of a murderer.

Outline of Text

In this chapter as the subject is introduced we cite the need that exists; the probability of murder in our present day society; statistics that represent individual lives rather than just numbers; an overview of the treatment program that has been developed for survivors of homicide in our community; and the choice of group therapy versus individual therapy to serve the majority of clients.

Guidelines are presented in Chapter Two which may be helpful to organize and design a treatment program for survivors of homicide. Chapter Three reviews the dynamics of loss, characteristics of normal grief and bereavement, and those issues which complicate the bereavement process for homicide survivors. Assessment and treatment issues are discussed in Chapter Four. Chapters Five and Six outline the design of the twelve session Group Grief Therapy Treatment Program which has been developed from experience with groups of survivors. This section was first written in 1985 prior to intake of the first group of survivors. After each session for the first three groups, the particular session was rewritten to meet the needs of survivors as they were conceptualized. This final draft may be rewritten many more times as we continue to learn. The appendices contain copies of documents found useful in development of the Homicide Survivors Group, Inc., of Pinellas County (HSGP), Florida, program. It is intended that the clinician may be able to make use of these documents in development of similar programs.

Rationale

We have a population of bereaved survivors who have been forgotten mourners for decades. Most therapists, mental health professionals, psychologists and psychiatrists have had little to no training in working with psychological trauma due to sudden, intentional, unexpected death. It is the *INTENT* of the act of murder, the willful disregard for life, that evokes such a traumatic reaction. The nation recoiled in horror at the murders of John F. Kennedy, Robert Kennedy, and Martin Luther King, Jr.. We showed concern for their widows and children. But what happens to the bereaved survivors of the thousands of other murder victims? In what manner have we cared for these forgotten mourners?

Little attention in our society has been given to the experiences of the surviving family members and friends of a murder victim. The family and friends of murder victims have become those for whom we have not developed programs of treatment. This population is ignored in our psychological literature. When the HSGP program was being developed, one paper was offered in the search of literature provided by the Library of the National Institute of Medicine. This was an evaluation of a six-session group program held in Hartford, Connecticut in 1981 by Katharine Miller, Nancy Moore, and Charles Lexius (1985). The group was open ended and provided an educational and support format for groups of homicide survivors.

Many bereaved homicide survivors report being told by professionals, "Just get on with your life." Some were placed on heavy anti-depressants, sedatives and sleep medication for years. Others were given Electric Shock Therapy for the depressive symptomatology of grief! Survivors have reported telephoning mental health services and being put *on hold* while the receptionist goes from doorway to doorway asking, "Does *ANYBODY* know *ANYTHING* about murder?" Hearing the repulsive comments of practitioners, the receptionist reports, "We can't do anything for you here!" One survivor kept an account of her requests. She telephoned 14 different offices requesting help. Another survivor found herself being treated by two graduate students who were not available at Christmas because their university course was completed. Many report the feeling that they must care for the therapist in reaction to their story of horror. Professionals need to change these practices and subsequently provide quality care for the survivor who has been traumatized by murder of a loved one.

The bereaved survivor is not just another statistic. To put this into perspective we must examine how our society has condoned murder and largely ignored the vast population of bereaved survivors which the act of murder leaves behind.

Crime and the Criminal

We witness a pornography of violence in our living rooms on television daily. Crime, criminals, the sight of a body bag, conjectures about the criminal mind, questions of why the murder occurred, explanations about early abuse and poor role models, and the scene of handcuffing the perpetrator and hauling one off to jail are frequent occurrences in the media. There is a daily menu of murder on each network station and in every newspaper in the country.

We are entertained by the mystique of the psychopathic deranged crazed mind, the pathological killer, *the perfect crime,* all depicted in television drama, art, and literature. Who among us has not viewed "Murder, She Wrote," a television drama, among dozens of other intriguing murder mysteries?

As a nation, we are intrigued with the mystique of these pathological activities. The media makes these stories commercially viable and we watch. The virus of information spreads, which may not only be infectious but psychologically damaging. The tendency is to glamorize crime and the criminal, and to degrade the profiles of victims. The press cannot be sued for libel by the dead. We are fascinated and entertained by stories of murder.

Research studies abound pertaining to what causes the criminal to kill. We have investigated every facet of prevention, prison populations, early release programs, rehabilitation and dozens of other issues related to the criminal. Yet, in the United States in 1988, over 20,000 murders occurred! The figure increases yearly. The Green River Killer alone may be responsible for the murder of over 200 young women. The following figures reveal the statistical probability of murder victimization in the United States in a lifetime (Uniform Crime Reports, 1986).

PROBABILITY

CLASSIFICATION	PROBABILITY OF LIFETIME MURDER VICTIMIZATION
U.S. Total	1 out of 153
Male	1 out of 100
Female	1 out of 323
White Total	1 out of 240
Male	1 out of 164
Female	1 out of 450
Non-White Total	1 out of 47
Male	1 out of 28
Female	1 out of 117

The probability exists for one of us out of every 153 persons to be murdered! And for a black male the probability of death by homicide is unconscionable!

Number of Murders

The Uniform Crime Reports for the United States in 1986 states that the number of deaths due to non-vehicular homicide is 20,613. That is 56 every day; at the rate of over 2 per hour. These are figures for the intentional, willful act of killing another human being. These do not include figures for accidental deaths or drunk driving fatalities.

Number of Survivors

With all the statistics we have available about the number of murders committed, the probability of who will get murdered, and the host of information on criminals, there has been little available information on the number of mourners left behind when a loved one has been murdered.

In working with over 300 families of murder victims, a genogram has been drawn of each family system (Redmond case file). From that documentation, the average number of mourners for each murder victim includes seven to ten surviving family members. These are members who are experiencing acute and chronic long term grief reactions. In just one year between 210,000 to 300,000 persons are identified in the population of homicide survivors!

To understand the implications of these numbers one must recognize it may take up to seven years for our criminal justice system to litigate the case. This is for all appeals to be heard and to not deny the defendant any of his legal rights under our constitution. Survivors repeatedly experience an acute grief reaction on each occasion the case is brought before the court. They are unable to work on grief or work through a resolution until the court has made a final ruling on the case. There are severe emotional reactions as one rehears and relives the circumstances of the murder in the courtroom. So in effect, homicide survivors live in a clouded world of grief for years after the murder occurs. And each year as our number of homicides grow, a disproportionate number of persons join the ranks of victim survivors in the emotional process of grief.

Homicide survivors report that they must, "put their grief on hold" because emotional energy is not available to deal with both the court proceedings and emotional rigors of grief work. This differs from the delayed grief reactions that clinicians see in other types of unresolved grief. In other delayed reactions, the griever is not aware of the cause of presenting symptomatic behavior. This is not true of survivors of homicide. Theirs is an intentional repression. However, the reactions are difficult to work through because they have been repressed. The source and date of problems can be identified which led to the presenting symptoms of dissolved marriages, family disruption, problematic acting out behaviors of children and adolescents, drug abuse and alcoholism, loss of work-related goals, loss of friends, and dysfunctional family systems.

Broad Field of Mourners

The count of seven to ten grieving affected members in each family system does not include neighbors, friends, co-workers or others outside the family system. Homicide appears to leave a wider range of affected survivors than from deaths by other causes. Many others experience reactions to the psychological trauma of murder in a community, who are considered to be outside the immediate circle of family members and friends.

Surviving members in the basic family unit, including mother, father, son, daughter, brother, sister, wife, husband, and significant others, are often identified as the persons most directly affected by the murder of their loved one.

In homicide, this nucleus of members is widened to include all of the extended family members, ex-spouses and ex-in-laws, as well as significant others who may have befriended the victim before the death; children in a classroom where a random killing took place; witnesses and bystanders; or a neighborhood where the screams of the victim were last heard. The number of affected survivors in a homicidal death is much greater than in deaths from other sudden unexpected causes.

This phenomena of increased numbers of mourners can be explained in part by analyzing cause and effect rationale. Our educational systems have taught us to examine causes and effects of any issue we cannot comprehend. The mind searches for a reason to explain how and why this atrocity occurred. When one is unable to understand the reason for the murder and must accept this as a random act, the mind continues to search for a cause. Lack of finding a cause leads one to fear for one's own safety, developing feelings of vulnerability, and exhibiting heightened anxiety and guilt over what could have been done to prevent the occurrence of the death. More people feel responsible and consequently outraged for the lack of prevention rendered than in deaths from other causes. The close family members of a suicide victim may experience greater personal guilt feelings than homicide survivors, but the overall number of survivors who are grief stricken by murder appears to be greater.

The psychological trauma of murder leaves lives shattered. Until recently, survivors have had little help in reestablishing a future life. Historically, murder has been a stigmatized death that few mental health professionals have examined in detail. However, an interest in the field of victimology has recently arisen throughout the nation in response to the demand and need of thousands of victims. This recent interest is a direct response to the rise in the crime rate, the no longer silent voice of the victim, and the persistence of the researcher who in some instances is a homicide survivor.

National interest has been directed to victims of crime by formation of several major organizations. The National Organization for Victim Assistance (NOVA) in Washington, D.C., was begun by Dr. Marlene Young in 1975.

Parents of Murdered Children (POMC) was formed by Bob and Charlotte Hullinger in 1979 as a self-help group of mutual supporters. These, along with the National Victim Center in Fort Worth, Texas, founded in honor of Sunny von Bulow by her children in 1985, have led to establishing a network for those interested in providing services to a vast field of victims of crime.

Communities throughout the country have developed programs similar to the Homicide Survivors Group, Inc. of Pinellas County, Florida (HSGP). Some programs are operational in the Office of the State's Attorney and include services to victims of all types of criminal victimization. Others are trauma specific and were organized as non-profit organizations to meet the needs of one segment of victim survivors similar to HSGP. An overview of the HSGP program developed for survivors of homicide in Clearwater, Florida, will clarify the design of that program.

Homicide Survivors Group, Inc. of Pinellas County

The program was developed to meet the specific needs of survivors of homicide. The goals outlined at inception were as follows:

1. Provide a group grief therapy treatment program for families and friends of murder victims.

2. Provide individualized psychological care to meet the specific needs of survivors, including educational materials and support.

3. Instruct two psychotherapists in clinical skills for each treatment group provided to survivors. Two mental health professionals from each local mental health agency are selected for training.

4. Provide educational and informational programs to the community to raise awareness of the needs of those victimized by murder of a loved one.

The HSGP program presently offers the following services:

1. Twelve-week Group Grief Therapy Treatment Program provided to homicide survivor groups. (10 members per group)

2. Individual counseling alone or in conjunction with group therapy when appropriate.

3. A Mutual Support group whose membership is open to survivors who have completed the Group Grief Therapy Treatment Program.

4. A Volunteer Training Course provided to selected volunteers.

5. An educational and clinical skills training course program in group grief therapy for homicide survivors is provided to two mental health professionals, in each group treatment program for survivors.

6. Educational programs provided to concerned community organizations throughout the year.

7. A national quarterly newsletter directed to concerns of survivors.

An overview of the order of services HSGP provides will be useful in visualizing the process of care for each individual homicide survivor.

OVERVIEW

HOMICIDE SURVIVORS GROUP, INC. OF PINELLAS COUNTY

ORDER OF SERVICES

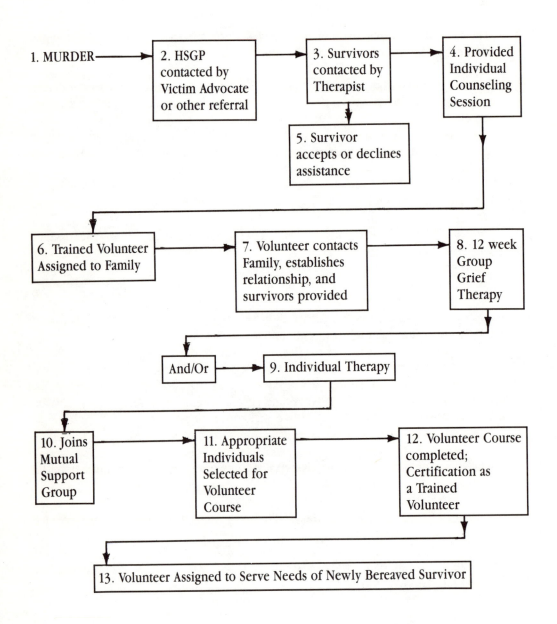

The progression of services is as follows:

1. The murder occurs.

2. HSGP may be called by victim advocates, Office of State Attorney, or law enforcement officers. Referrals are frequently received from other homicide survivors, physicians, attorneys, or other sources.

3. The survivor is telephoned by therapist and offered assistance. Program and services are described. An appointment is scheduled if appropriate.

4. An assessment intake session is provided. Support and assistance given. Written educational materials are provided.

5. The survivor accepts or declines assistance. If survivor declines assistance, educational materials are sent out by mail. The name is placed on a waiting list in case of a later request.

6. A trained volunteer is assigned to a family who will be the primary source of support for the first 2-3 months.

7. The volunteer contacts the newly-bereaved family and plans individual intervention based on needs of survivors. The needs of the family are reviewed with therapist.

8. The Group Grief Therapy sessions are provided, if appropriate.

9. Individual therapy may be the treatment of choice for first 3-4 sessions prior to group, or may be provided instead of the group program when appropriate.

10. The survivor may join the Mutual Support Group after completion of Group Therapy Treatment Program.

11. Survivor volunteers are selected for Volunteer Training Course after successful completion of their own therapy program. The purpose of this selection is to prevent a survivor who has personal unresolved grief issues from overloading a newly-bereaved survivor with the volunteer's issues.

12. Volunteers who complete the six-week 12-hour Volunteer Training Course are provided certificates of completion.

13. The cycle is repeated as the new Trained Volunteer reaches out to assist the newly-bereaved.

The HSGP program was developed to meet the needs of survivors of homicide. The following needs have been defined:

NEEDS OF SURVIVORS

1.   To become empowered and gain control of one's life.

2.   To gain support in an environment where survivor is free to express one's self; (cry, talk, scream, laugh, be angry, shameful, guilty, fearful, etc.)

3.   To gain acknowledgment of the loss by supportive others.

4.   To know and understand the design and purposes of associated systems (law enforcement, criminal justice).

5.   To integrate the murder into one's mental framework.

6.   To work through the grieving process and achieve resolution as emotionally stable as possible.

Three modalities of treatment which have been utilized to meet the needs of survivors are: individual therapy, group therapy, and mutual peer support group. It would be useful to consider the different goals and values of each modality.

Individual Therapy

van der Kolk (1987) relates that most trauma victims benefit initially from individual therapy. HSGP survivors are first seen in an individual screening intake session. Individual therapy allows for disclosure of the trauma, the safe expression of related feelings, and the establishment of a trust relationship with at least one other person. The survivor gains a sense of control as one relates the impact the murder has had on his present life, and the pain is acknowledged. Horowitz (1985) noted the need to alternate between support and confrontation so the client can cover up traumatic material when it threatens to overwhelm him yet not wall off the constriction of affect. Individual therapy allows for a detailed examination of mental processes and personal memories not possible in a group setting. The survivor gains the undivided attention of the therapist.

However, individual therapy can lead to dependency on the therapist who may be seen as having all the answers. The survivor may look to the therapist rather than within oneself for solutions. Those who may be inappropriate for group therapy, and are seen only in individual sessions, must be encouraged to foster relationships and reconnect with others in the community. The individual's strengths must be explored and tested, and accomplishments praised.

Many of the HSGP survivors are provided three to four individual sessions prior to the group treatment program. This allows establishment of a secure relationship and reduction in the intense search to find all the answers in the experience of the group.

For those who are judged inappropriate for group therapy, eight to sixteen individual sessions may be required to work through the psychological trauma. Some of those who have been determined as unsuitable for group treatment are: a Nazi Germany war survivor whose parents, siblings, and grandparents were killed in the holocaust; a paranoia schizophrenic widow whose husband was murdered; a mother who was given 10 Electric Shock Therapy treatments six months after her 19-year-old son was stabbed to death; and survivors who demonstrate borderline personality character disorders.

Group Therapy

van der Kolk (1987) documented group therapy as the treatment of choice for psychological trauma. This modality has been used successfully in rape, child and spouse abuse, death-related bereavement reactions, and other traumas. The loss of a sense of connection to society can be restored as the survivor relates to a group of fellow sufferers. There are three phases in the group process: the orientation phase, a conflict phase and a sharing working phase.

In the orientation phase, the group members use one another as mirrors to reflect traumatic memories and feelings, providing a shared reliving of the murder event. In making the past public each begins to find a sense of shared loss. A sense of community develops as members share their horror and other group members do not withdraw their emotional support. A mother whose 24-year-old daughter had been killed said, "Before I came I had no reason to believe you would be any different than others. I went to a psychologist who said, 'I have to put it behind me'. Even when I tried to tell her what it was like to clean up my child's blood that day, she changed the subject. Here, you cry with me, and listen, so now it's not so important to talk about it anymore. You let me tell it."

In the conflict phase an internal power struggle is evident in an effort to determine how much to share intensely personal material. Subsequently, a sharing working phase develops with open sharing, reliving personal memories, and developing trusting relationships. The group member begins to develop a sense of control as one experiences himself in the role of caring for others.

The experience of being both victim and helper provides flexible roles of passivity (being dependent on others) and activity (providing support to others). Group therapy is less likely to foster dependency. Issues are more easily confronted and addressed by at least one member of the group from whom the others gain introspection relating to their own similar issues. Symptomatic behaviors are better explained and understood, while thoughts and feelings become progressively normalized more quickly in the group environment.

The goal for group leaders is to coordinate and lead each group member into individual confrontation and resolution of unresolved grief issues. During therapy the major tasks are to create and maintain cohesion, guide and direct the focus on grief issues, and prevent constriction of affect. Timing is essential. There is a time to explore at a more complex level and a time to allow emotional distancing. Confrontation too soon or too abrupt can be overwhelming, and may lead the survivor into total withdrawal. Grief therapy is a carefully directed slow process and must not be rushed. The proverbial ball of yarn unwinds slowly.

Mutual Peer Support Groups

Mutual support groups are provided to *SUPPORT* the survivor, not to resolve conflictual issues as in therapy groups. The group is therapeutic but is not therapy. Highly anxious individuals who expect to resolve conflicts in an ambivalent relationship with the deceased will be disappointed in this modality. Toxic issues cannot be addressed. Affect may be constricted due to unresolved grief and significant unpleasant past memories. Mutual support groups are not appropriate for everyone. Some survivors cannot bear to hear of the trauma in others lives without feeling too overwhelmed to carry on with their own burden. Others express dismay when they hear of murders that occurred 5-10 years earlier and learn that the peer is still struggling to integrate the trauma into his life. If exposed to either a peer support group or group therapy too soon after the trauma, the survivor may withdraw and abandon further contact.

Osterweis, Killilea, and Greer (1984, p.274) in assessing the value of treatment modalities for the bereaved suggested that "...Although numerous anecdotal reports and a few controlled studies attest to the positive features of mutual support, it is possible that peer pressure exerted on individuals who are psychologically vulnerable could lead to some poor outcomes, such as feelings of failure for not living up to group expectations or changing in ways that, although consistent with group norms, are ultimately not helpful to the individual."

In mutual support groups, behaviors and topics which are expected, appropriate, and socially acceptable are addressed. Symptomatic behaviors can be understood and normalized. This is an excellent format to acknowledge the pain of loss and gain knowledge of other systems. A peer group following the therapy group provides a bridge back into social relationships and a greater sense of community. The griever who has expended emotional energy working through the grief process in therapy now has energy to expend in the development of new relationships. This is found in the peer group as a supportive environment encourages the transition back into the community.

Individual Sessions For Others

To clarify the services of HSGP, individual sessions may be provided to others who do not need the 12-session format provided in the Group Grief Therapy Treatment Program, nor extensive work in individual therapy. One family member may request assistance for the family system, come into therapy 2-3 times, be provided informational materials, and return again six months to a year later during the court trial period. Not all of the family members come into therapy or request assistance. Members are identified by use of a genogram with the presenting family member. Many are sent informational materials or are provided telephone counseling on request. Young children may be seen once or twice. Parents are taught how to work with their children to alleviate and understand grief manifestations and the way children behaviorally act out the pain of grief. All children are given their own appointment card and an invitation to telephone for assistance whenever needed. Many 6-10 year olds telephone to report their progress and just to visit with an understanding therapist. Children are seen in subsequent visits when appropriate.

Training of Professionals

The reader may use the materials suggested in the course work for training of group co-leaders. Eight therapists have been trained in HSGP by the clinical director. Those who are familiar with death education materials and have developed counseling skills in working with the bereaved will respond to the challenge of this learning experience.

In the therapists preparation to lead and develop a treatment program for survivors of homicide, it is helpful to review literature on group dynamics and group process. The review of Yalom (1975) and others in the field of group therapy provided insights which proved helpful prior to development of the first HSGP pilot project group.

The course work requires a minimum of 60 hours. The clinical work in group therapy requires 24 hours, 2 hours per session for 12 sessions. Co-leaders and the instructor meet 1/2 hour before and 1/2 hour following each session for pre-and post- group sessions. Homework assignments will require at least 2 hours of study per week.

One of the prerequisites in the 60-hour course work is completion of the required reading prior to the screening intake session of the homicide survivor. This includes:

1. J. William Worden, (1982) *Grief Counseling and Grief Therapy.* This book details the differences in these two therapeutic forms and provides an excellent goal-oriented model from which to proceed.

2. Therese A. Rando, (1984) *Grief, Dying, and Death: Clinical Intervention For Caregivers.* This material brings into sharp focus many facets of the subject matter.

3. Bessel A. van der Kolk, (1987) *Psychological Trauma,* "The Role of the Group in the Origin and Resolution of the Trauma Response." This chapter explains how the group becomes therapeutic, the role of the leaders, and the process by which resolution is achieved.

Reading and writing assignments for the clinician are outlined after each session of the Group Grief Therapy Treatment Program. Those clinicians who achieve all assignments will be better prepared professionals and more capable in handling the complications of the homicidal bereavement process. The course requirements and study questions for professional therapists are outlined in Appendix C.

The following exercise is required of clinicians in training. Prior to proceeding, take the time and effort to assess personal death related experiences. The practitioner who gains self awareness of one's attitudes, values, and beliefs will be better able to assist those one serves.

HOMICIDE SURVIVORS THERAPY GROUP

Preparation of Therapist

We, as therapists, are mortal human beings. We have developed death-related attitudes, feelings, and fears similar to the bereaved survivors whom we strive to serve. Kavanaugh (1974) urged us to become aware of our responses for effective work with the dying and bereaved.

The following is an exercise adapted from work by Therese A. Rando (1984, p.9) to assist us in self-awareness. She states, "Our early experiences with loss and death leave us with messages, feelings, fears and attitudes we will carry throughout life. To prevent our being controlled by our unconscious and conscious reactions to past experiences, it is important to recognize and state explicitly how these experiences have influenced us and our lifestyles."

Early Experiences and Recent Experiences

1. What was your first death experience? Who died?

    a) When did it occur? How old were you? Who was with you? Who else was involved? What happened?

    b) What were your reactions? List those you believe to be positive. List negative reactions.

    c) What were you advised to do, and what did you do to cope with the experience?

    d) Who was most helpful to you? What occurred that may be hurtful?

    e) What did you learn about death and loss from this first experience?

    f) Of the things you learned then, what makes you feel anxious or fearful now?

    g) Of the things you learned then, what makes it easier to cope with death now?

2. Think about your next death-related experience.

    a) When did it occur? Your age? Where was it? Who was involved? What happened?

    b) What were your reactions? Think of positive and negative aspects.

    c) What were you advised to do, and what did you do to cope with the experience?

    d) Who was most helpful? What did they do? Who was hurtful? What did they do?

e) What did you learn about death and loss from this experience?

f) Of the things you learned then, what makes you feel anxious or fearful now?

g) Of the things you learned then, what makes it easier to cope with death now?

3.   Think of your most recent death experience. Repeat the questions asked above.

4.   Of these three experiences, do you see any reactions that form a pattern?

a) List the repetitive feelings, attitudes, and beliefs.

b) How do these feelings and attitudes about death affect how you currently cope with loss experiences, positively and negatively?

c) How does your interest in working with bereaved survivors of murdered victims relate to your personal issues on death?

Socio-Cultural, Ethnic, and Religious/Philosophical Attitudes

Reflect on your socialization and on attitudes about murder in our society. Think about your beliefs regarding the victim, the murderer, the surviving family members, friends, the criminal justice system, media representation, and support systems.

Think about issues regarding afterlife, burial rites, expected attitudes of loved ones before and after the murder, expected fears of the victim, expected differences in reactions to death by murder, expected differences in age and gender of deceased and survivors, attitudes toward caregivers, and attitudes toward children.

1.   Write out attitudes held by your colleagues toward death by murder.

a) Your socio-economic group.

b) Your religious/philosophical/ethnic group.

2.   Which norms, mores, beliefs, sanctions, and attitudes have you internalized about death by murder from these groups?

3.   How might these cultural beliefs and attitudes affect the ways in which you work with bereaved survivors of homicide?

After completion of these exercises, arrange to meet with your co-therapist and group leader for a discussion on the above.

The next chapter presents the organizational design of a program for the private practitioner who is contracted by a private organization or who desires to establish a program within one's own practice.

*"Some men see things as they are and say 'Why?' I dream
things that never were, and say, 'Why not'?"*
George Bernard Shaw

CHAPTER TWO

Organization and Design of Program

There are many organizational tasks when formulating plans to establish a group treatment program for survivors of homicide. Some tasks are outlined below with a description of the experience of establishing the Homicide Survivors Group, Inc. of Pinellas County (HSGP). This outline may provide some helpful guidelines but is not all inclusive. Assistance received from the community, state agencies and national organizations will be invaluable.

Needs Assessment

A written needs assessment will provide factual data. Those who work in law enforcement, victim advocacy, the criminal justice system, and mental health agencies will be helpful in documenting the needs that exist. Members of local chapters of organizations such as The Compassionate Friends, Parents of Murdered Children, and Mothers Against Drunk Driving will also be helpful in providing data. Statistical facts to support program planning can be obtained from The National Crime Survey prepared by the U.S. Department of Justice, Bureau of Justice Statistics, and The Uniform Crime Reports of the Federal Bureau of Investigation.

The needs assessment includes:

- number of murders that occurred in last year in your community
- number of murders in last five years
- approximate number of affected survivors
- level of care being provided at present
- competency of professionals providing care
- availability of professional resources in the community
- projected need for services and cost
- cost in terms of psychological damage without program

Community Awareness

To obtain the support and commitment of the community they must be informed about the factual data gathered. They will need to know about the normal reactions of survivors of homicide and the psychological trauma as a result of murder. If there are no trained providers of care in the local mental health agencies, the community must be made aware of that fact. Local community leaders may expect that survivors are receiving psychological care and not know services may not exist. Topics such as Post Traumatic Stress Syndrome and Grief Therapy have not been offered as part of the curricula in most institutions who train mental health professionals.

Attempt to include personnel from the mental health centers in early planning. Local mental health agencies may be interested and helpful but unable to support a program due to lack of personnel or funding restrictions. Mental health agencies become a major source of referrals and should be kept informed of progress of the program. Professionals from the agencies may volunteer and be selected as group co- leaders. This broadens the network of care for survivors.

A completed needs assessment becomes the basis for a written proposal to be presented to local community groups. The proposal must include the professional qualifications of the proposed provider. Copies of original proposals prepared for Homicide Survivors Group, Inc. of Pinellas County may be found in Appendix E and F.

Informing The Community

Upon completion of the needs assessment and proposal for the development of a program, prepare a formal presentation to present to community groups. Providing education to community organizations and leaders will help reveal availability of additional resources, and emphasize the commitment to expanding the scope of services that exist.

Copies of the proposal may be mailed to community organizations with an offer to present to the membership at one of the organization's regular meetings. The Chamber of Commerce can provide a mailing list of organizations from which you may select the most appropriate groups. The proposal for HSGP was mailed to 100 local organizations in 1985. Thirty-three organizations responded and were provided presentations.

Presentations to community groups may be made by a professional therapist and one homicide survivor. The professional presents the factual data, reveals the need for psychological care, and resources presently available. The homicide survivor may give a personal account of the circumstances of the murder of his or her loved one, and the need for emotional support and therapeutic intervention. This account will document the lack of available services presently available, the support provided, and subsequent effects on his or her family.

Support of Victim Advocates

The victim advocates working in local law enforcement and the state attorney's office are the foundation of professional support for a treatment program. No one is more aware of the need for services. The victim advocates work daily with victims of all types of crime. Their professional responsibility is to keep victims informed, assist in obtaining services from community resources, and provide assistance throughout criminal justice proceedings. Victim advocates will be a major source of referrals for the treatment program.

HSGP would not have formed without the commitment provided by the victim advocates of the Pinellas County Sheriff's Office. The advocates approached mental health agencies seeking training for mental health professionals, documented the need that existed, and were present at all meetings to enhance the design and progress of HSGP.

Support of Victim Rights Community Groups

Major support for the establishment of the treatment program can be achieved through local groups interested in the rights of all victims of crime. The director or a representative of all the social service organizations in the county form the membership of the Pinellas County Victims Rights Coalition, Inc. (PCVRC). Many of the major counties throughout the nation have similar organizational groups. The group provides a network of support for each program directed to assist victims of crime. It is important to share early planning with the group and keep them informed of progress and development. The PCVRC assisted in early fund raising efforts for the development of HSGP.

Support of Public Mental Health Agency

Public mental health agencies must provide psychological care to a large segment of the population. Agencies are frequently disadvantaged due to a lack of trained personnel, restriction of funds, and overload of demands for services. Mental health professionals will be able to assist in documenting the need for services. They also may become avid supporters in development of a program.

Support of State Agencies

The Health and Rehabilitative Services (HRS) in Florida or similar agencies in other states may be approached for support and funding. Although the state agency is diverse in its scope of services provided, it is the foundation of the health care delivery system for the vast public sector. State funds are difficult to obtain since they must be budgeted and approved by the state legislature. This is a path which is time consuming and requires infinite political acumen. It is a difficult task. It is speculated that ten years from now most states will provide some level of funded services to survivors of homicide. Similar to the hospice movement, it will require the efforts of thousands of victims in a grass roots movement informing individual legislative delegates of existing needs.

In Florida, The Florida Network of Victim Witness Services, Inc. provides a network of victim service providers. Local, regional, and state seminars and conferences are held to provide education and training to volunteers and professionals in all victim of crime interest groups. Local state network organizations will be helpful in providing contact with other professionals throughout the state, in disseminating information about the treatment program, and providing a referral source for the program.

National Organizations

There are several national organizations which are available to provide education, training, and support for the design and implementation of a treatment program.

The Association for Death Education and Counseling, Inc. (ADEC) provides workshops which lead to the national certification of death educators and bereavement counselors. Membership in ADEC provides the therapist a directory of members which is a network of other professionals and lay persons involved in death education and counseling.

A newsletter published six times a year contains the most current information in thanatology. Recent research in the field of thanatology is presented at annual conferences which are held in various locations throughout the country. For those who may be interested in certification in death education or death-related counseling, ADEC provides a certification program for professionals and associates (see ADEC reference).

The National Organization for Victim Assistance (NOVA) in Washington, D.C., has designed training programs for victim advocates, prosecutors, law enforcement, workers in the criminal justice field, mental health professionals and administrators of programs for victims of crime. NOVA has established a Crisis Response Team of trained volunteers which responds to national tragedies, such as airplane disasters, mass killings, or other major traumas. The library staff at NOVA assist in researching documentation on other programs, exchanging information, and referrals. NOVA provides assistance in legislative issues and testimony to federal government agencies documenting the needs of victims of crime.

The National Victims Center, an advocacy and resource center founded in honor of Sunny von Bulow in Fort Worth, Texas, provides training and technical assistance throughout the United States. The Center's library and resources are among the best in the nation to help victims and advocates find information and assistance from over 6,100 local, state, and national victim service programs. The National Victim Center is particularly noted for its training programs in working with the media, the criminal justice system, and local, state and national networking.

Parents of Murdered Children (POMC) was founded by Charlotte and Bob Hullinger in Cincinnati, Ohio, in 1978, three months after their daughter, Lisa, died from injuries inflicted by her former boyfriend. This is a self-help organization providing support and guidance to bereaved survivors. Educational programs provided at the POMC national conference assist others in forming local chapters. There are local chapters organized throughout the United States.

Mothers Against Drunk Drivers (MADD) has made a national impact on legislative issues toward the prevention of vehicular homicide on our highways. MADD has maintained a focus on the issue of drinking and driving. High school students have formed chapters of Students Against Drunk Driving (SADD) which offer programs teaching prevention in high schools throughout the nation.

The Society for Traumatic Stress Studies was formed in 1985 by a group of leading professionals in the field as a way of assuring that information in this relatively new area of scientific inquiry and professional practice would be shared as widely as possible.

Since its establishment, over 1,000 mental health, social service, religious, and legal professionals have become members of the Society. Members include professionals who work with veterans of combat, victims of crime and other forms of violence against persons, survivors of natural and technological disasters, refugees, Holocaust survivors, victims of torture and political violence, persons suffering from duty-related stress, and individuals who have suffered other forms of physical and psychological trauma.

Three organizations, The National Organization for Victim Assistance, Inc. (NOVA), The Society for Traumatic Stress Studies, Inc. (STSS), and the National Victim Center, Inc. (NVC) are designing a tripartite National Certifying Board. This board is working toward the development of certification of Trauma Counselors in victimology.

These are the major national organizations which complement one another and work closely together to form an alliance of resources for the provider of services in the field.

Funding

This may be one of the most difficult problems in planning to provide a treatment program for survivors of homicide. It is important to make use of local resources and community support to fund a pilot program for 10-12 survivors.

HSGP received the first contributions from the League of Victims and Empathizers, Inc. (LOVE), of Palm Harbor, Florida, a grass roots organization founded in 1982 by Wendy Nelson. LOVE was formed to provide support for victims of crime and help achieve changes in state legislation after the murder of the Nelson's ten-year-old daughter, Elisa. The LOVE members provide Court Watch in all homicide cases in the local court system and accompany victim survivors throughout the proceedings. Other helpful organizations in the formation and development of HSGP were the local chapter of The Forum For Death Education and Counseling, Inc., and The Junior League of St. Petersburg, Inc., who provided the remainder of funds required for the HSGP pilot program.

The pilot program establishes a basic level of services for survivors. Homicide survivors who complete the first treatment group provide a core of supporters who may assist in securing other sources of funding.

The first group of homicide survivors who completed the HSGP treatment program vowed to assist in making it possible that every survivor in our county would have access to the type and quality of services they had received. The HSGP program has been developed from the results of that first pilot program through the work of volunteers and professionals.

During the second and third years of operation HSGP has been funded by a grant from the U.S. Department of Justice, Office for Victims of Crime, which supports efforts at the federal, state, and local levels to assist victims of crime and administers the Victim of Crime Act (VOCA, 1984) funds. The revised VOCA Act of 1988 extends crime compensation funding for six years and includes a mandate to aid "underserved victims of violent crime." Homicide survivors have been categorized as a population of underserved victims in the 1988 VOCA Act. The state Bureau of Crime Compensation and Victim Witness Services provides the administration of VOCA funds for local state programs.

DESIGN OF PROGRAM

The implementation of the plan for the treatment program will be more easily achieved with the supportive network of local, state, and national organizations in providing educational resources, guidance, and direction. The design of the program must be adjusted to meet the local needs of each community. Copies of documents which were useful to develop HSGP are included to assist in development of individual program designs.

The HSGP statement of purpose, outline of objectives, statement of need, population at risk, resources and funding, and other general information may be used as guidelines for the program proposal (Appendix E and F). The Organizational Plan format may be useful in the organization of the treatment program (Appendix G). Charts show the growth and development of the HSGP program.

Service Providers

HSGP was designed to provide psychological care under a licensed mental health professional. The services of a licensed physician, who is a practicing psychiatrist familiar with complicated bereavement issues, were engaged in order to achieve an initial referral source and provide primary supervision.

Clients who may need psychotropic medications are referred to the psychiatrist who is familiar with the case from the supervisory sessions. HSGP chose the physician as the Medical Director on the HSGP Board of Directors. The physician is informed about the program direction and lends medical credibility and expertise.

Supervision is obtained at the mid-point and end of the group treatment program. Also, the psychiatrist is readily available by telephone for consultation which may be advised during the program. The group co-leaders serving in the position of trainees are required to attend and report to the psychiatrist on the progress of the cases at the supervisory sessions.

Selection of Therapists

One of the goals of HSGP was to close the gap in services unavailable to survivors of homicide by the local mental health service delivery system. Education and training of mental health professionals who were employed in local agencies was the method chosen to accomplish that goal. The program was designed to select two therapists from each mental health agency in the county. Two therapists receive clinical training in the role of group co-leaders for each group treatment program of 10-12 homicide survivors.

The mental health agency must be made aware of what you as a provider can do for them. If you plan to train their personnel, specify what the training program will consist of, what qualifications are required for therapists to be trained, and what the cost in time and money will be to the agency. A written contract signed by the director of the agency that has been reviewed and accepted by the agency's board of directors will minimize complications. A three-year "non compete" clause may be included in the contract. This will provide the opportunity to train therapists from several agencies without duplication of services.

The Mental Health Services of Upper Pinellas, Inc., who supported the pilot project which formed HSGP acknowledged the existing need for services for survivors of homicide and provided two therapists to be trained from their agency. The therapists were selected by the agency based on their supervisory and teaching roles within the agency. This plan was developed in order for the therapists to be able to subsequently teach other counselors within their own agency through inservice training programs. Therapists in private practice may also be selected when deemed appropriate. It is the practice of HSGP to select only qualified state licensed service care providers as trainees.

The decision to train no more than two therapists in each group of 10-12 clients was based on the necessity of not overloading the group with therapists. The availability of at least two therapists at all times is assured with assignment of a group leader and two co-leaders for each group treatment program. If one of the three therapists cannot attend a session, two co-leaders are still available for the group session.

One of the problems that exists in selection of therapists is to choose those who have the recommendations of the agency to study the materials, complete the assignments, and devote the clinical time necessary with survivor clients. Sponsoring agencies must understand in advance the level of commitment required from them to permit the therapist in training sufficient time away from normal job duties toward this effort. Selection of trainees who have a background in death education studies and previous experience in bereavement counseling will alleviate some of the work overload.

Another problem to consider is the frequency of staff turnover in agencies. Once a therapist is trained in a particular agency, and that staff person leaves for another position, the agency is left without the resources of the trained qualified therapist.

Group Leaders

The leader must meet with co-leaders to review course requirements, roles, and functions for each of the positions. Joint decisions are made cooperatively on meeting times, selection of site locations, and other logistical details.

Meeting Location

The choice of a meeting site for the group will be dependent on the availability of appropriate places in each community. The selection of a library conference room, school, or public building proved successful for HSGP until a home office was established. A degree of privacy must be maintained to encourage free expression of emotion. The HSGP office contains a large group room arranged to provide a therapeutic environment.

Experience in working with grieving survivors reveals that it is preferable not to locate the group meeting site in a mental health center or a church-related setting.

Unfortunately, our society recognizes a negative connotation when referring to mental health agencies who, by practice and design, offer emotional support, guidance, and counseling. Persons assume the stigma of *mental illness* not mental health for those who frequent mental health agencies. The surviving family members of murder victims are overwhelmed with their own feelings of *craziness* and will resist this form of further victimization by hesitating to attend a program in a mental health center. Several survivors have reported they did not tell other family members they were attending a group until they could establish their own sense of sanity and personal safety. Furthermore, those who do not have their own transportation do not want a neighbor, friend, or relative to drop them off at a mental health facility. This is not the time or place to debunk the myth of who should seek services at mental health facilities. A psychologically sound treatment program can be located at many varied locations.

Many survivors will also resist attendance if the group meets in a church-related setting. Many survivors have experienced a difficult time in accepting a violation of their religious beliefs. Some do not feel that the church was there for them when needed most. Also, regardless of what church building might be selected, there are others who are not of that belief or faith who will feel abandoned. After therapy, many survivors report a renewal of their faith and belief system and again attend the churches of their choice. From experience, it is suggested not to interfere in that expressly personal choice.

Age and Residence Requirements

HSGP has restricted the group treatment program to adults over 21 years of age. This is based on the established knowledge of patterns of bereavement for adults as opposed to those of children in bereavement. It is planned in the further development of HSGP to offer group therapy for children and adolescents.

HSGP has not restricted participation by a residence requirement. It was decided that county residents would be given first priority but those in adjoining counties who seek therapy are provided access to the group treatment program.

Brochure

A brochure will need to be designed to inform the public of the program, objectives, meeting time, dates, location, and contact persons. Brochures may be disseminated through all the public agencies, criminal justice system, law enforcement offices, libraries, hospitals and physician's services. The brochure is helpful in notifying the media and may result in extensive media coverage and subsequent referrals.

Media Coverage

A review of materials in the National Victim Center manual on meeting with the media will enhance the presentations provided to radio, newspaper, and television audiences. A contact with media representatives should be planned at three-month intervals and prior to the start of each new group treatment program.

Referrals

Referrals will be received from every agency in the community, particularly from the victim advocates who work in law enforcement and the state attorney's office. Contact with local police departments, attorneys, mental health care providers, and the media will provide a major source of referrals.

In Chapter Three, patterns of normal grief and bereavement are presented, followed by a discussion on the complications of homicidal bereavement.

*"Death is not the greatest loss of life
The greatest loss is what dies inside us while we live."*
Norman Cousins

CHAPTER THREE

Grief and Bereavement

This chapter provides a brief discussion of concepts of loss, examines the normal process of mourning, and symptoms of grief which occur as a normal reaction to all types of death. Then, some of the complications of bereavement due to the murder of a loved one are presented.

CONCEPT OF LOSS

The British psychiatrist, John Bowlby (1977) has devoted most of his professional career in the development of theory concerning attachment and loss. His attachment theory provides a method for us to conceptualize the need in humans to make strong affectionate, emotional bonds with one another, and to understand the depth of the reaction when the attachment is threatened (severe illness) or broken (in death).

Humans develop attachments early in life to meet the need for *security and safety.* The attachments are directed to a few individuals and endure throughout most of one's lifetime. Bowlby regards attachment behavior as distinct from the biological needs for food or sexual behavior. When the bond is threatened, a normal biological reaction occurs to protest, seek, and restore the attachment. We can think of examples of the baby who protests mother's leaving and pines by the window until her return, only to show anger when she enters. The hospitalized child often shows crying, clinging, angry outbursts when parents leave. Searching and seeking behaviors ensue. If the child is successful in getting the parents to remain, the child no longer feels threatened, the emotional need is satisfied and the stress is alleviated. Worden (1982) relates that if the need is not satisfied, apathy, withdrawal, and despair are evident.

We witness examples of this phenomenon in infants who fail to thrive, whose need for bonding and trusting another has gone unmet. Later, this child often has difficulty in establishing trust with another human being and may display angry acting-out behaviors. The failure-to-thrive-infant is grieving for the loss of an emotional attachment and cannot trust that others will provide safety and security. Each of us experience the crisis of loss throughout our lives. We search to replace, restore and readapt to the changes brought on by the break in our attachment to the object or person.

A common denominator in all crisis is loss. We grieve for our losses, whether they are the loss of a treasured timepiece, loss of a camera, loss of our possessions through purse snatching, loss of a home and possessions from fire, loss of a loved relationship by estrangement or divorce, or the ultimate loss of a loved one by death. Furthermore, there are multiple behaviors — physical, emotional, cognitive, and social in each loss situation. Think of your reactions the last time an object was misplaced. Did you search? Review in your mind the last time you saw it? Think where you may have had it? How you used it? Did you get angry at yourself or others for not being able to locate it? You were trying to reestablish a connection with a lost object! Normal reactions to loss are compounded by what meaning the object held for you in your life. When it is the irreplaceable loss of a human being, the loss of a person for whom we have an emotional attachment, we experience multiple normal reactions of grief.

Each loss results in the need to do "grief work," as it was labeled by Lindemann (1953). Mourning the loss is that painful process of preoccupation with the lost object or person. Caplan (1962) suggests that, if one is to survive the losses suffered in a tragic crisis, one must hold up the image of what was, reviewing in detail, reviving memories of what life once had been. Only then, can one begin to accept the change and begin the process of resolution.

GRIEF AND BEREAVEMENT

Bowlby (1980) explains that grief is a normal reaction of protest engendered to restore the lost relationship. There are biological, psychological, physiological and social responses to the effort to retrieve or reestablish a relationship with the lost object.

George Engel (1961) described grief as a deep painful psychological wound similar to the trauma one sustains in a severe physical wound. Grief work, the resolving of the relationship, is analogous to scar tissue laid down to nurture and close the wound. Because grief work is so painful, mourners may suppress their emotions in an effort to stop the pain. In effect, a bandage or cover is laid over the new raw open wound, leaving the wound without oxygen, to fester rather than to heal slowly.

Envision a deep penetrating open raw wound with bloody jagged edges. If one chooses to avoid the painful experience, withdrawing from the pain and trying to go on with life without dealing with the wound, it tends to abscess; sending up sharp unrelated angry outbursts, painful relationships, irritable behaviors, depression and other symptomatic behaviors. One must go through "grief work," grieving for one's losses, in order to heal the wound. The work of grief therapy is to debride the wound, scraping the internal edges clear so that healing may begin to take place. Scar tissue will be laid down as the wound heals slowly from the inside. When the wound is healed there will be a scar but it will be a *healed* psychological wound.

"GRIEF IS THE KERNEL OF ALL PSYCHOPATHOLOGY!" This profound statement was made by Norman Paul at the International Conference on Grief and Bereavement in London,

England, (1988). If one can accept that grief is the seed of psychopathology, we can understand the importance of going through the mourning process and accomplishing a healthy resolution to our losses. This becomes the very basis of sound preventive mental health care.

MOURNING PROCESS

The process of resolving conflicts imposed on us by death is called mourning. Bowlby and Parkes provide four helpful descriptive phases of the mourning process: 1) shock and numbness; 2) yearning and searching; 3) disorientation and disorganization; and, 4) resolution and reorganization (Davidson, 1979).

All four dimensions are usually present when the mourner learns of the death. There is an ebb and flow, highs and lows in the process, there are no neat dividing lines between the characteristics. As the mourner begins to resolve conflicts of the loss, feelings of shock and numbness pass; there is less searching and yearning; disorientation and disorganization appear less frequently; and the mourner reorganizes to learn how to relate to the world without the deceased. It is the *resolution of the conflicts* brought on by the death, *not the passage of time* by which the mourner achieves resolution of the process. *Time alone does not heal.* For those who avoid grief work, time does nothing but pass, leaving grievers to deal with unresolved, delayed grief reactions which may become exaggerated and complicated. However, it takes time to resolve the many changes in one's life brought on by the death of a loved one. Grief work may dominate the life of a mourner for the first two years following a death.

Shock and Numbness

Immediately upon news of the death, the mourner feels stunned; there may be outbursts of intense panic, distress and anger directed toward those present. Functioning is impeded. Decision-making is difficult and concentration is limited. A protective psychological numbing occurs as the defense mechanism of denial protects the ego. Mourners describe feeling as though they are encapsuled within a heavy plastic shield, observing others in an unreal world. The mourner remains distant from others, feels vulnerable, and is protective of self. When the psychological shock is so severe as occurs in unexpected deaths (accidents, suicide and homicide), there may be no memory of what was said or done. There is a loss of emotional connection within the mourner, and between the griever and the outside world. Attention span is short at the time when crucial, objective decisions must be made, such as funeral arrangements and estate settlement. Characteristics of shock and numbness appear to be most intense in the first two weeks but may peak again on the anniversary of the death or at other trigger points in the life of the bereaved.

> The police telephoned Mrs. K. to identify her murdered sister. Outside, the morning was bright, sunshine flooded the trees and birds were singing; inside the house was a scene of horrible slaughter of a beautiful girl. Later, Mrs. K. related, "seeing this detective who was directly in front of her, move his lips as though he were talking to her for the longest time." She heard nothing he said. She remembered, "the feel of the sunshine and the sounds of the birds."

Davidson (1979) explains that the basic conflict of the tension between the reality of the *IMMEDIATE PAST* and *IMPOSED PRESENT* is characterized by resistance to stimuli. A display of what appears to be inappropriate emotions such as laughter at a funeral or stoic acceptance without emotional outbursts may be misinterpreted by onlookers. The mourner may be unable to comprehend or interpret the meaning of the event and may display inappropriate emotions.

Searching and Yearning

The mourner may have the fear of *going crazy* — as one hears, sees, or senses the presence of the deceased. The mourner is sensitive to the habitual sounds and sights associated with the deceased. These searching and seeking behaviors are normal reactions to loss. Reports such as hearing the deceased's car pull into the driveway; sounds of the key in the door latch at the usual homecoming time of day; seeing the deceased in a crowd at a mall; feeling the hand of the deceased on a shoulder may be normally described during this period. The mourner may forgetfully set a place at the dinner table; then hurriedly remove the setting for fear of being discovered by other family members and be regarded as emotionally ill. One fears for one's own sanity. The mourner may be overwhelmed with feelings of anger, self-blame, and guilt. Davidson (1979) explains that during this period the mourner is testing what is real. Equilibrium cannot be restored until reality is established and understood. Searching and yearning behaviors appear to be most intense from two weeks to four months following the death, but may reappear again around the anniversary.

> A father whose 16-year-old son was killed in an automobile crash spoke of how, "Each night when I come in from work, I go into the kitchen to see what kind of homework Bob brought home; it's not until I'm standing in that empty room that I know he is not ever going to be doing homework or anything again. Somehow, I forget for moments or just can't let myself believe it."

Disorientation and Disorganization

The mourner feels disorganized, depressed, guilty and unable to accomplish normal tasks. Disorientation appears most intense from the fourth to sixth month following the death. By this time friends, other family members, and co-workers may voice the expectation that the mourner *should be* over the acute grief. The opposite is true. The mourner feels more pressure from the expectations of others, while at the same time experiencing heightened anxiety over an inability to organize thoughts and actions.

This is a time the mourner most needs the support of others. Physical symptoms of stress appear. Complaints may vary from cold symptoms, flu, tiredness, and insomnia, to a range of psychosomatic illnesses. Physicians, without a careful assessment may diagnose the symptoms as clinical depression, rather than part of the mourning process. Contrary to popular opinion, anti-depressants and tranquilizers are not appropriate for treatment except in rare circumstances. These drugs may mask the symptoms and lead to a long-term unresolved grief reaction.

Harry, 44, a divorcee, requested individual grief therapy. He was a physician who was experiencing a severe acute grief reaction to the death of his 14-year-old son who had lived with his mother. On intake Harry revealed he had been placed on heavy doses of tranquilizers since his divorce five years earlier, and had increased the consumption of medication since the death of his only child four months earlier. Grief therapy was hampered by the medication and proceeded very slowly as a result of unresolved conflicts of the divorce which were more predominate than conflicts due to the death of his child. This presents a case of multiple losses and unresolved relationships, with the most recent psychological assault resulting in complete disorganization.

Disorientation is the result of the piercing awareness of reality clashing with the imagery of what is desired and life as it once had been for the mourner. The confusion results as the mind refuses to accept the present reality, but must live in a reality without the presence of the deceased. The emotional anxiety and stress on the body triggers the physical symptoms. This may be one of the most dangerous periods for suicide contemplation for the bereaved. The characteristics of disorganization are a necessary part of grief work and lead into progressive adaptation and integration of the loss.

Those who desire to help can be most effective by listening to the mourner's feelings related to the reality of the loss. An adolescent expressed guilt and suicidal ideation because she now had her older deceased sister's nicer room and her wardrobe, and enjoyed them. This is part of the reality of death; rooms and clothing are used by others. By expressing these emotions the adolescent was better able to accept the changes as reality, and express her sadness felt due to her sister's death.

Resolution and Reorganization

For an adult mourner four characteristics which appear to dominate between the 18th to 24th month after death are:

1. A sense of release from the loss of the loved one.
2. A renewed energy that can be confirmed by observers.
3. Ability to make judgments and handle other complex problems.
4. A return to eating and sleeping habits the mourner had before the death of the loved one.

The intensity of the loss is still great and memories associated with the deceased are still present but the major focus of one's life becomes future oriented. Grief may be experienced in sharp painful moments many years later but be of shorter duration, with less frequency and intensity.

Regardless of the type of death the loved one suffered, these normal reactions of grief are experienced by all mourners in varying degrees. The following outline of normal symptoms of bereavement was adapted from Worden (1982). This proves helpful in educating the mourner that grief has recognizable symptoms and may dominate the mourner's life for a longer period of time than expected.

SYMPTOMS OF NORMAL GRIEF

Physical

Tightness in chest

Tightness in throat

Oversensitivity to noise

Depersonalization

Breathlessness

Weakness in muscles

Lack of energy

Dry mouth

Hollowness in stomach

Sighing

Treasuring objects

Behavioral

Sleep disturbances

Appetite disturbances

Absentmindedness

Social withdrawal

Dreams of deceased

Avoidance of reminders

Searching/Calling out

Restless overactivity

Crying

Clinging to reminders

Emotional

Shock/Numbness

Sadness

Anger

Guilt/self reproach

Anxiety

Loneliness

Helplessness

Yearning

Emancipation

Relief

Cognitions

Disbelief/Denial

Confusion

Pre-occupation

Sense of presence

Auditory and Visual
hallucinations

SUDDEN DEATH

When the death occurs from sudden, unexpected circumstances, such as a heart attack, accidents, suicide or murder, bereavement reactions may be more severe, exaggerated, and complicated. The coping mechanisms of the mourner may be overwhelmed. This is not meant to indicate that grief is not painful regardless of the type of death, or that one bereavement reaction is more severe than another. But that other factors may impinge leading to a more complicated bereavement. Variables which influence the individual's reaction to bereavement and a discussion of survivors of suicide and accidental deaths are in the following chapter in the treatment issues section. Since the focus of this book is on those who survive the willful intentional act of murder of a loved one, those factors which complicate the bereavement reaction for homicide survivors will be discussed.

COMPLICATIONS OF BEREAVEMENT

There are varied reasons for the delayed, exaggerated and complicated bereavement reactions experienced by survivors of homicide. Major characteristics experienced by survivors are cognitive dissonance, disbelief and murderous impulses, conflict of values and belief system, and withdrawal of support due to the stigma of murder. Survivors must deal with feelings of fear and vulnerability, anger, rage, shame, blame and guilt, and emotional withdrawal. The lack of familiarity with and support by law enforcement, the criminal justice system, and media intrusion also lead to bereavement complications. The delays in resolution of the murder conviction, lack of adequate punishment for the crime, and lack of acknowledgment by society heightened the feelings of loss of control.

Each of these present as treatment issues in working with homicide survivors. The ones selected for this discussion are those most commonly reported and expressed by survivors in individual and group sessions.

Cognitive Dissonance

At news that someone you love was murdered, the first reactions of disbelief, shock and numbness are apparent in the inability to accept the news as real. Remarks such as, "It can't be," "Oh, my God, no," are indicative of the denial mechanism. There may be claims that the informer must have made a mistake, denying that this could happen to a loved one. There is no preparation for this sudden onslaught. There is no comprehension that death could come so swiftly, and in a violent, degrading, brutal manner at the hands of another human being.

The death does not make sense; the mind cannot comprehend the meaning. The mind demands more information than can be processed or stored. Questions about events leading up to the murder will be asked repetitively, seeking both understanding and confirmation that it is not true! Nothing in our coping mechanisms prepares us for this level of psychological trauma.

Jim, a father, had been part of the search party looking for his missing 14-year-old daughter for over 24 hours. The fire department discovered her mutilated body in a burning shack. Months later, after the funeral, investigations, arrests and pre-trial hearings, Jim continued searching. He circled the same locations covered in the original search. He cognitively knew that his daughter was dead, but "I could not believe that she was really gone."

The mind is overloaded with the events prior to, during, and after the murder. There is a constant rehearsal of events; what happened; when; how; where; who did what; and the unanswerable, but *WHY?* There may be questions that have been answered in a logical sequence by law enforcement officers, victim advocates and other officials. None of the answers are *good enough*. The mind is searching to understand something that is incomprehensible. The act of reordering the events in order to understand takes much longer than we may expect. This cognitive dissonance may continue for months or years, and may be triggered by the court proceedings or other events relating to the murder for years in the form of a delayed grief reaction.

Murderous Impulses and Anger

One of the most difficult emotional reactions to understand by survivors, family members, friends, therapists and others who serve the victimized survivors is the intensity, duration and frequency of anger and rage. Anger is a normal healthy emotion. Lifton (1979) describes the paradigm of the emotional state of anger on a continuum from anger to rage to violence. To *fantasize* acting out rage is normal. To act out rage is violent behavior and must be prevented.

For the homicide survivor, the normal anger of grief is compounded by the rage and desire to violently destroy the murderer of the loved one. The psyche is dominated by images of what the survivors *would, could and should do* to the murderer. Elaborate plans of torturous treatment may be devised. The images of seeing the murderer suffer in a more horrendous manner than one's own loved one suffered are normal reactions for the murder victim's survivors.

Frequently the survivor is ashamed to tell anyone of the horror of the retaliatory thoughts. It is not unusual for the victimized survivor to fantasize painful castration of a rapist murderer followed by a slow bleeding death. Lifton (1979) explained that anger has to do with an internal struggle to assert vitality by attacking the other rather than the self in order to prevent a sense of inner deadness.

A 68-year-old father whose son had been murdered fantasized the opportunity to slice the accused murderer's body just enough for him to bleed lightly, then trolling him as bait through shark-infested waters. He was so ashamed of these retaliatory thoughts that he withdrew from his family in deep depression.

Survivors are frightened by their murderous impulses and their sense of rage. They ask themselves, "Am I no better than the one who killed my loved one?" "If I know myself to be a good person, yet I feel the desire to castrate, mutilate, or degrade another human being, can I really be a good person?'' Further, ''If I could do such harm or think of such savagery, am I safe around my own family?'' This can lead to emotional withdrawal and deep depression. ''I must be going crazy'' is a common response of survivors. The survivor should be reassured that he is not *going crazy,* that such retaliatory thinking is quite typical and expected under the circumstances. The internal conflict with one's own sense of values, beliefs, and sense of justice is overwhelming. The murderous impulses to attack the other in retaliation for the pain suffered by the murder victim, and the pain of grief of survivors must be explored, exposed, and understood during the therapy process.

It is in venting and verbalizing the murderous impulses that the anger begins to lose some of its intensity and power. The thoughts do not have to be acted out when one can tell the fantasy and the therapist listens with acknowledgment, understanding and non-judgmental acceptance. Verbalization and ventilation provides a path to reframe the scenario, it is a way to rehearse what in effect could, should and would be done. Lifton (1979) explains that the imagery serves to define one's troubled existence. The discussion of violent imagery serves as a form of restraint against it being misguided into actual violence. As therapists, *we must NOT BE FRIGHTENED OF LISTENING TO IMAGERY OF RAGE!* Recognize that the professional's understanding of this concept is crucial to the therapeutic process. A therapist must be prepared to experience this venting of anger and understand the normality of this behavior.

Lifton (1979, p. 151) states that ''The release from the anger, rage, violence paradigm will be dependent on the capacity to accept one's inactivation under the circumstances.'' Most survivors are able to release anger, bitterness, despair, helplessness and frustrations as they examine what can be accomplished. This becomes a focus of the therapist's work in *empowering* the survivor. The survivor is empowered through knowledge of the normal and expected symptoms of grief, by gaining knowledge of the entire circumstances of the case, and knowledge of what can be expected of the criminal justice and other related systems. The painful reactions are normalized. There must be acknowledgment by others that the sense of powerlessness and frustration is real, painful, and a common characteristic.

It is not unusual to see survivors displace anger. The anger may not be directed at the criminal, but at others who surround homicide survivors. Targets of this displaced anger may be family members, friends, co-workers, strangers in the street or even those who are trying to assist. The threshold level of instant irritation and self-control is low and survivors do not have the internal controls to endure even slight irritations.

In a *stranger-to-stranger* crime, the survivor and defendant have little to no contact. Anger, pain, fear and violation become more real when the offender is caught and brought to trial. Survivors at trial are amazed at their own restraint. They must endure the pain of visually seeing this human being face-to-face. In contrast, if the offender is never apprehended, then he or she becomes a *mystical figure,* elusive and not entirely real to the survivor. There is greater cognitive dissonance because there are more unanswered questions to internalize. Questions which can only be answered in the imagination.

A young woman, whose mother was murdered four years ago by an unknown killer, recognized her anger and irritation over the slightest offenses. She said, "I see the murderer in every place I go, in the mall, driving down the street, in the grocery store. I was getting mad and taking it out on everybody. Once I was able to understand the anger I began to direct it, I don't have to be mad at everyone else, just the invisible killer."

In therapy groups survivors are asked, "What do you want to do with your anger?" It is the survivor's emotion and has the powerful ability to transform negative trauma into positive accomplishment, but the choice must be up to them. This technique is not useful until the anger has been verbalized, explored, reframed, rehearsed, and exhausted. It must be the survivor's choice whether it will be part of an internal dialogue for the rest of one's life. By offering the survivor this choice in decision making it adds to a sense of being in control and reaffirms one's power.

Fear and Vulnerability

Survivors express a pervasive sense of fearfulness and apprehension, feeling vulnerable to further psychological or physical assaults. The fears are not irrational. The world is no longer safe as was previously believed. Parents restrict remaining children, worry about business or personal travel of other loved ones, and restrict their own activity. A mother of a 10-year-old murder victim reported that five years after the murder, her two elderly aunts, who live together, will not answer the telephone after 3 P.M., they no longer go to concerts or social events, and live in fear of someone else in the family being murdered.

Frank, in his mid 40's, finds he must search through every room of his home when he returns home from work daily. His father was killed in the family home. Jeff, another survivor, bought a gun after the murder of his daughter. He had never used one before but slept on it under his pillow for months. He said, "I simply cannot let anything else happen to my family, I'm scared to death but if I am going to be killed . . . , I must protect the other children."

Chronic phobic reactions can develop and lead to total dysfunction due to paranoia and a sense of vulnerability. Following a presentation on normal grief and bereavement to a self-help support group for agoraphobia, a young 18-year-old came up afterwards with tears running down her cheeks. She said she had been in a mental hospital for over a year after her brother's murder. She felt this was the first time she could understand what may have happened to her. She described her paranoia, depression, suicidal ideation, and subsequent emotional withdrawal. We can only question if grief therapy may have changed the course of this young life? Fear must be expressed and examined for an orientation to reality. Bard (1986) relates that by providing ventilation these feelings will begin to diminish in intensity, duration, and frequency.

Conflict of Value and Belief System

Murder violates our belief that we have a right to life and is in direct opposition to the high value we place on life. In other deaths the crisis may unite a family of supportive survivors. However, frequently in homicide, the effect of murder results in explosive reactions destroying interpersonal relationships between survivors. (Further information on explosive and cohesive families is contained in the rationale section of session six, Chapter Five). Each member searches for a reason for the sudden, unexpected, intentional act of destruction of the life of their loved one. This is a personal violation for each one's value and belief system. We value life and believe if we are good people, do not hurt others, and practice our Judeo-Christian beliefs, that life and God will be fair to us. Murder is a violation of everything we have been taught to be right, honest, fair, or expected in life. Each person searches to understand an act committed against their individual beliefs. When unable to comprehend or understand, they feel powerless, frustrated and without hope. They may question what is of value, if not life? What other parts of my belief system are false? What else have I been taught to believe that is fraudulent and untrue? It is a lonely, individual search for understanding. There is a loss of trust and faith in the world as it was believed to be.

Members of the family withdraw from one another, each nursing one's own level of psychic pain and grief. The level and intensity of grief will differ for each. Individuals experience feeling states unique to their personality, coping mechanisms, previous crisis experiences, support, and individual relationship with the deceased, and, one's relationship within the family. Each experiences emotions of guilt, anger, fear, anxiety and vulnerability. The anxiety in the system is turned up full blast, similar to the volume on a radio, and the noise ricochets in every thought, feeling and behavior of each family member. Anxious systems do not behave like calm ones.

In an effort to regain some sense of control, survivors experience guilt, blaming themselves or others for some word, act or deed that was done or undone. The thought that one may have changed the situation, time, place or circumstances to prevent the murder is often apparent. When the family system blames one of the surviving family members, either verbally or non-verbally, or when one member accepts blame, the entire relationship system may deteriorate.

Guilt and Blame

Guilt is intricately embodied with a sense of control and the search for a reason for the death. An understandable explanation is necessary for the mind to absorb the meaning of the victimization. The assault is internalized and the barrage of "if only's . . ." is endless and treacherous. We seek to blame others or ourselves in order to make sense of the tragedy and to confirm a sense of control over our life. In the Grief Experience Inventory post test of group members, 18 out of 28 showed a marked reduction in feelings of guilt; 4 who showed a reduction in guilt revealed a marked increase in the loss of control components with 12 showing no change (GEI evaluations, see Chapter Six). This is a small sample to confirm a correlation but is indicative of the relationship between guilt and loss of control.

We have been taught to be responsible for our lives, activities, careers, care of our children, care of ourselves and those we love, and believe we have the power to control the destiny of those responsibilities. Survivors express guilt and feelings of responsibility because they believed themselves to be in control and were, in fact, in control prior to the event. There is incongruity in this belief as it is proven invalid after the murder of a loved one. The criminal has erased the power and control exercised in carrying out the daily functions of living. The murderer not only took the life of the victim, but plunged the lives of the survivors into excruciatingly painful grief.

Frequently, one parent may blame himself or herself for any deviation that may have taken place in an otherwise normal routine. What the survivor is saying is that, "I am responsible for this, I made it happen." If the survivor does not think of this primarily, someone else may direct blame either verbally or nonverbally. At times the survivor assumes he is being blamed by others, when this is not true. However, to verbally confront the issue with others becomes an overwhelming burden.

In the death of a child, parents may go to great lengths to assuage the guilt of the other parent. But the sense of being protected from blame is a heavy burden for the one who feels guilty. This is a major cause of marital relationship problems following the death of a child. Expressed feelings of shared guilt have a therapeutic value.

> Jane allowed her 15-year-old daughter off disciplinary restriction to attend a neighbor's party. She finished the dinner dishes, primped, and as she was leaving, her father grinned and kidded about, "how easily she could convince Mom to have her own way." Mom did not tell Dad she had also granted an extra 30 minutes at the party.
>
> Their daughter was assaulted, robbed, raped and brutally killed that night after she left the neighbor's home. Father silently blamed mother for allowing her off restriction and himself for not demanding compliance with the disciplinary decision. Mother blamed herself for the 30-minute extension. Neither parent ever spoke of their inner feelings to one another. It was not until Jane sought professional help for her suicidal ideation three years later, that she revealed this burden of guilt. She had been so ashamed, it had been impossible to reveal it to anyone.

Family members may give or accept unrealistic responsibilities for a crime. A husband or father may assume an inordinate level of blame because he failed to protect his family. Survivors may also blame the victims for *allowing* themselves to be murdered. In our society men have traditionally been raised to be *our protectors*. One of the crucial differences in the grieving process for men and women is how much greater the level of unspoken guilt is present in males.

The degree of blame and guilt can be intensified if the murder occurred during the time the relationship was undergoing a stressful period or incident. If the murder occurs immediately following an argument or family altercation, the magnitude of unresolved grief will be more severe.

Even when no blame exists within the family, each family member may begin a process of withdrawal from one another, protecting one another, the youngest members or the elderly from the gruesome facts of reality. Communication becomes inhibited and strained as each feels isolation and a deep sense of personal emptiness.

Stigma of Murder

In our society, we have held the belief that those who are murdered have in some way led to their own death. Members of a community in which a brutal murder has taken place will often blame the victim or survivors. This is again, the same search for a reason to be able to comprehend the horror. By these explanations, a protective shield is set up within the mind of the observer that the circumstances are such that the tragedy would never happen to them. Everyone is, in reality, vulnerable to victimization but will seek security in finding components of the criminal activity that *could never* occur in their life. A superficial aura of personal security is established to counteract this real vulnerability.

An internalized sense of personal security is exhibited by onlookers as victims are labeled *bad, drugged, careless, seductive, promiscuous, with the wrong crowd or, in some manner, asked for it.* Families of victims are also stigmatized because it is believed that they should have stopped the behaviors blamed on the victim, or at least have expected the traumatic outcome. It is as though what is being said or thought is, "If I blame you for 'letting' your child be killed, how can I still be your friend?"

This is irrational thinking on the part of others to prevent acknowledgment of their own vulnerability and the randomness of murder. Evidence of this fact is reflected when it is the murder of an innocent child or an elderly woman or gentleman.

In order to prevent our own loss of control and gain understanding, we project blame on the lack of parental care, other caregivers, or the system within which the victim was a member. The mind continues to search for explanations until it becomes accommodated. In this projection of blame, the observer finds comfort and accepts that one's family is exempt from such a horrendous tragedy. This type of rationale provides emotional distance, and exclusion, protecting those who are neighbors, friends, co-workers, and other community members. This type of thinking and reactive behavior by others leave the survivors alone in their sorrow.

It is the emotional distancing of others and stigmatization that leaves the survivors of homicide feeling abandoned, ashamed, powerless, and vulnerable. Survivors report not receiving sympathy cards, the inability of others to even say "I'm sorry," or co-workers inability to acknowledge absence from days of work. Examples of these types of sensitivity to the needs of others are acknowledged freely in other types of deaths. Survivors report the sound of whispers among co-workers, recognition that the murder case is the subject, but lack of acknowledgment that it is their murdered loved one under discussion. Friends, who do not know what to say or do, become uncomfortable and withdraw emotional support.

Many survivors report that cherished friendships become dissolved at the time of murder of their loved one.

When the surviving family members acknowledge that there were predisposed circumstances, such as drug abuse, which may have led to the murder, this does not lessen the intensity of the loss to the survivor. Ambivalence creates the opposite effect. Those who have opposed parental or spousal wishes do not deserve to be murdered! The survivor must subsequently endure not only the loss of the loved one, but the death of personal hopes, dreams, and unfulfilled expectations that perhaps someday the son, daughter or spouse would have functioned in a more productive lifestyle. The survivor experiences a greater sense of personal failure when there is ambivalence in the relationship, and the process of bereavement becomes more exaggerated and complicated.

Intrusion By Other Systems

The raw wound of the grieving homicide survivor is overtly and covertly affected by the performance of law enforcement officials, criminal justice practitioners, media personnel, and others after a murder. Prior to the murder, there is a lack of knowledge and familiarity with the functions of these systems in the normal everyday life of victim survivors. After a murder, each system intrudes in the most personal matters in one's life at a time of great emotional turmoil. Many describe secondary victimization as more severe than the psychological trauma of murder. This is due to the intrusion by outside others, lack of knowledge, and lack of familiarity with the systems and the belief that the systems will represent the rights of crime victims. This often does not materialize.

Law Enforcement

Law enforcement officers may be sensitive and gentle but, as part of their duties, bring the most devastating news one can ever imagine. The message that "someone you love was murdered" is so harsh, ugly, devastating and unthinkable, that notification of next-of-kin is a horrendous task. No matter how the message is conveyed, the memories of those moments will be etched in the mind of the survivors forever. Surviving family members frequently remember the exact words used, how the officer looked, the number on the police badge, the way one stood or even held their hat. Some survivors physically attack the news bearer, scream, run, or faint. The desire and need to lash out in rage at the bearer of bad news is more than understandable.

Previous personal experiences with a police officer may be only limited to receiving a traffic ticket. Suddenly law enforcement takes on a different meaning and unfamiliar impact in the survivor's life.

The griever is in shock and may not understand the words. Survivors may want more information than the investigating officer can share at that time. The survivor's defense mechanism of denial may be shattered by an officer who does not understand the psychological protection of the denial mechanism. The event is not only fraught with anxiety and psychological trauma, but is an intrusion into the personal, private, inner core of one's existence. In order to assist those who must provide death notification, Janice Harris Lord, (1988) Director of Victim Services at MADD National Headquarters, has outlined excellent suggestions for death notification to be used by police officers and others.

When one or more family members are suspected of the murder, there are additional complications in the bereavement process. The family system is shattered by the incongruency of grieving for the victim and loyalty to the defendant. There is a compounded loss of the loved one to murder, and the accused to a term of incarceration.

Criminal Justice System

There seems to be an endless list of new words, phrases and roles in the unfamiliar world of the criminal justice system. The majority of people have never dealt with an attorney in their life. Suddenly thrust into the role of victim survivor, they must learn the meaning of the related terms and roles of personnel such as: victim advocates, prosecuting attorneys, defense lawyers, investigations, hearings, pre-trials, plea-bargain, continuances, court dates set and postponed, judges, court reporters and others.

The survivor finds out the charge of murder is a crime against the state, not against the husband, wife, mother, son or other for whom the survivor grieves. One may be required to give a deposition on the pretense of being a witness by the defense attorney when, in fact, this often turns out to be a ploy of the defense to keep them out of the courtroom. The prosecutor may plea bargain, allowing reduction of the charge to a lesser offense in order to get a conviction; and this may not be discussed, explained, understood, or agreed to with surviving family members. Victim survivors often have to face the defendant in the courtroom or in the corridor or waiting room. It is traumatic to come face-to-face with the murderer of a loved one. There may be numerous trips to officials' offices requiring days off from work, lost wages and the ire of perhaps a less-than-understanding employer. Families may travel long distances incurring expenses to attend a trial that is delayed with no notification to the family of survivors.

Exclusion from the courtroom or remarks such as, "You should just get on with your life," "Leave this to us," or "Why put yourself through that?" discount the importance of the role of the victim and survivors. Survivors who are not present at any of the hearings or proceedings feel left out and abandoned by the system believed to provide justice for those who suffer at the hands of criminals. They must know they had the opportunity to represent their loved one no matter how difficult the court experiences.

In court, survivors may hear reports of early *good boy* school records, testimonials from teachers, principals, church leaders, boy scout masters, neighbors, friends and family members who testify for the defense of a known killer. It is not unusual to observe a jury, judge and society as a whole adopt the attitude that the victim must be to blame for one's own death. The victim survivors may have to contend with release of the criminal, light sentences, the crime never being solved, the crime not prosecuted for lack of sufficient evidence, or presented to a grand jury and not prosecuted with subsequent release of the murderer.

The murderer, whom one testified against in a trial, might be released on a work release program unknown to victim survivors. The fear of retaliation for testimony that led to conviction is real. The list of secondary victimization by the criminal justice system appears endless. As a professional therapist, one may hear bizarre accounts of insensitivity and incredulous stories of victimization by the courts.

> The mother of a murder victim said, "I could deal with the murderer, I knew he had to be sick to do such a terrible thing to my daughter, what I have had the hardest time accepting is the way the system has treated us. There's *MORE* frustration and pain in dealing with the system, than with the murder. There's one closed door after another. Everyone tells you what you can't do: *can't* come into the courtroom, *can't* show any emotion in the courtroom, *can't* get a trial date set, *can't* get a first degree murder charge. My worst victimization was by our criminal justice system. I needed to be in that courtroom, I needed to see the pictures of her body, and understand how she had fought him off. They wouldn't recognize my ability to make those decisions for myself." It has been repeated many times, "The first rape was by the rapist, but the worst rape was by our systems of justice."

Media

Although a large portion of crimes such as child abuse, sexual assault, rape, and spouse abuse are under-reported crimes, when they are reported, the victims have the privilege of being treated in a confidential manner. This is not true for victim survivors of homicide. Murder is an act against the state that usually does not go unreported and survivors are identified publicly. There is no code of confidentiality for homicide survivors.

The sensationalism used by the media makes the stories of murder commercially viable. The sight of a body bag has quite a different meaning to surviving family members than it does to the majority of the viewing public. A microphone thrust into the face of a grieving mother asking, "How do you feel?", does not indicate the meaning, care or concern of an interested person. The media may ignore murder of low status victims and exploit stories of high profile victims.

Watzlawick (1988) wrote of Jean Baudrillard, a French sociologist's description of the obscenity of television. Baudrillard spoke of the brutalizing effect of pools of blood, pictures of beheaded accident victims, and violent crimes that have become the essential, if not the sole, ingredient of newscasts. Scenes like the shameless and disrespectful close ups of people in desperate and tragic emergencies, the mother holding the body of her dead child, the moronic questions fired at someone who really needs to be left alone. This is followed by the idiotic banter of a commercial and defended as the citizen's right to be kept informed under our constitutional law.

> Mrs. Caesar watched the scene of her 17-year-old daughter on television. Janie was missing and later found murdered with her ravaged body in a ditch. The shock

and numbness of grief did not protect the mother from the scene of her daughter's murder. She could not believe this was her child. She said, "Television is for entertainment and for celebrities, Janie would have loved to be on TV!" Other pictures of the high school beauty queen appeared counterfeit in the mother's eyes. In her stunned state, her child's photos appeared unreal. The nightmares became a daytime horror. After all, she pondered "Janie had never been on television during her life, why must she be in her death?"

Survivors may not know they have the right to refuse interviews by the press and television media. They may be incorrectly quoted. Also, they may find out details about the case which they never knew before from the 6:00 evening news.

More than one survivor has reported finding out about the murder of a sister, daughter, or husband from the telephone call of a news reporter. Others found out their missing loved one was dead after reading a daily newspaper.

Other Systems

Systems of health care may also be a source of secondary victimization to survivors. Victims may have survived for hours requiring extensive emergency surgery. Hospital personnel overloaded with their medical duties, dealing with the intrusion of law enforcement personnel into their system, often have difficulty providing compassionate care to families.

Even after the death has occurred, survivors report lack of knowledge of the patient's condition, being closed in a waiting area for hours with unanswered questions. Later, they find that the death of their family member occurred hours earlier, and they were not informed. One family reported that the hospital personnel denied that the patient had died, two hours later they were informed they could leave since the body of the victim had already been transferred to the medical examiner's office!

This in no way is meant to indicate that there are not kind, considerate, sensitive and caring personnel in law enforcement, the criminal justice system, the media and health care systems. Many were taught to utilize emotional distancing in order to handle the trauma and stress of their daily jobs. Some are seeking education in victims issues, and sensitivity training, in order to prevent secondary victimization to those they serve. The need to educate and train a vast audience is evident in regard to these issues.

Loss of Control

Americans and individuals in most western cultures cherish freedom and the right to control their own lives. It is believed that in order to succeed individuals must be in control. People make choices: where to work, live, worship, play; what education level to attain; how to raise their family; what rules and structure are most appropriate within their family; and how to achieve defined goals in their lives. Free cultures possess this defined right of freedom and expect to be able to direct their lives within the confines of the laws. We have referred earlier to how guilt correlates with loss of control. It is as though one says, "If I had not done something wrong, this would not have happened, because I am a responsible person.'' We cannot be responsible for the actions of others. However, when one believes he is in control and this is violated, feelings of powerlessness ensue.

When a crime occurs, the victim survivor becomes frustrated and powerless, control of one's person, property, or possessions are lost. A criminal takes command of the very personal and private right to control one's own life, possessions and lives of those whom one loves.

First, the criminal violated the inalienable right of the human body to life. This represents and engenders everything the victim meant to each and every one who knew him and loved him.

Then law enforcement and criminal justice systems control one's right to information, to search for the accused, to defend the honor of a loved one in court, or to seek justice through punishment of the perpetrator. Whatever level of justice is achieved is arduous and slow, and it requires constant vigilance on the part of survivors.

Loss of control becomes even more pronounced when the perpetrator is never apprehended, punished or acknowledged as at fault. In this event, the level of psychological trauma has no closure for survivors.

The normal state of confusion experienced by all who grieve is complicated by the introduction of unfamiliar roles, legislative rules, court activities, and unfulfilled expectations. Homicide survivors consistently report feelings of abandonment, loss of control, and powerlessness in greater frequency, intensity and duration than in any other type of bereavement reaction. They are more often required to put their grief *On Hold* until they have learned to cope with the intrusions of the outside world.

Emotional Withdrawal

Benign events may become the stimulus for aversive emotional responses. An exploratory study of 19 survivors by Amick-McMullan, Kilpatrick, Veronen, and Smith (1989) suggests that aversive responses by survivors may be due to classical conditioning theory. The profoundly traumatic threatening experience of being told of the murder of a loved one is likely to elicit powerful, unconditioned, unlearned stress responses. These include the physical, emotional, cognitive and behavioral symptoms previously discussed.

Later, the situation (e.g., a telephone ringing, a news report, or news of a scheduled trial date) becomes associated with the reactions experienced at the time of notification. An individual seeks to avoid those stimuli that elicit traumatic responses. Extinction could occur if a survivor were repeatedly exposed to a conditioned aversive stimulus (telephone ring) without that stimulus being paired with traumatic news. However, if the survivor avoided telephones, the aversive responses would have no opportunity for extinction. Survivors may develop avoidance behavior and isolate themselves through learned responses to avoid the aversive stimuli. It is not unusual for survivors to avoid helping professionals, and members of their family who have become reminders of the homicide.

Lindemann (1944), Krystal (1968), Lifton (1979) and van der Kolk (1987) have described the experience of uncontrollable severance of affective ties in psychological trauma. In the acutely traumatic state, one stands alone and loses all sources of feelings of security. There is a break with the continuity of life, an emotional separation from all one's emotional connections and experiences that have preceded the traumatic event. The bonds linking people together are shattered with a loss of the sense of commonality. This leads to disorientation, demoralization, and loss of connection. Survivors are often ashamed of their own fears and vulnerability. Erickson (1976) suggests that they become enraged about the lack of help from outside systems, and lose faith in the possibility of meaningful and mutually beneficial relationships. Survivors ask, "How could anyone ever understand how I am feeling?", "Who knows or cares?" and, "Why should they care?" There is a discounting of one's feelings as being unimportant, insignificant, and without value. A survivor said, "I feel as though life has been crushed out of me. I do not belong to anyone now. Even my husband can't understand me and I can't explain it."

The survivor withdraws to make sense out of the tragedy. There is no emotional energy to direct to others. And if there were, the survivor questions being worthy of assistance. The state of the survivor is analogous to that of the wounded animal who withdraws to lick one's wounds, retreating deep in the forest of one's own self imposed isolation.

The senses are constantly overwhelmed with guilt, shame, blame, anger, murderous impulses, fear, vulnerability, intrusive thoughts of the deceased, physical aching and longing, nightmares, and loneliness.

> When Betty came to group therapy, she had not been out of her upstairs bedroom except to bathe and eat for over a year since the murder of her youngest son. She had seen a psychiatrist twice who prescribed major tranquilizers.
>
> A year later she painfully began to resolve many of the issues of her son's death through the HSGP group therapy treatment program. After the treatment program, she became a major fund-raiser for a children's organization which required contacts throughout the community in schools, churches, and other organizations.

A major goal of therapy is to build a bridge back to the world of the living, recreating a sense of interdependency, so that survivors may reconnect with their families and community. One cannot accomplish this goal without *integration* of the experience into one's own psychic framework. The positive results of the group treatment program are clearly evidenced in the above case.

To further clarify the content of this chapter, it is important to recognize that the emotion of grief is a normal reaction to the loss of a loved one. There are normal cognitive, physical, emotional and behavioral characteristics of grief experienced by the bereaved. When the death is due to murder, the mourning process is exaggerated and complicated. The complications do not indicate this is a pathological reaction. On the contrary, the reactions discussed in this section are normal and expected in homicidal bereavement.

Untreated, the normal reactions to the abnormal event of murder, may lead to psychopathology. With treatment, survivors of homicide insure their right to an emotionally healthy, functional life. The work of the therapist is in preventive psychiatry. The focus of the work is to prevent normal reactions to psychological trauma from becoming a pathological pattern and a dysfunctional way of life.

Other major variables in homicidal bereavement are: the circumstances of murder, status of murderer, court experiences, and the availability and use of support systems. These variables are discussed as part of treatment issues in Chapter Four.

"What lies behind us and before us are small
matters compared to what lies within us."
Ralph Waldo Emerson

CHAPTER FOUR

Assessment and Treatment

The quote above was used on the first brochure designed for the Homicide Survivors Group. It speaks to the power within each individual, the indomitable spirit to keep going despite hardships, to accept changes in one's life which were never asked for but must be dealt with, and the ability to reach deep inside one's self and learn new coping mechanisms in the face of adversity. It is fitting as the mental health professional considers treatment issues which will serve to *empower* the homicide survivor. Neiderbach (1988) stresses that we must do no harm in our effort to help.

Included in the assessment section of this chapter is an outline of variables that influence the grief process, symptoms of post-traumatic stress syndrome, trigger events, and secondary victimization. Listed under treatment issues are the screening intake format, use of genograms in assessment, selection of group membership, information provided to survivors who have been screened as appropriate for the treatment program, the use of the Grief Experience Inventory instrument, release form information, fee schedules, the use of confrontation, reordering and renewal as therapeutic techniques, and other issues which must be considered in providing treatment.

ASSESSMENT

INFLUENCING VARIABLES

We have recognized that we all grieve for our losses. However, the intensity, frequency and duration of the process of grief varies for each individual. We do not all grieve alike. Grief experienced by two family members for the same victim will be different because each one had an individual relationship with the deceased. Grief is as individual as a person's fingerprints. There are many variables that influence the way one responds to the death of a loved one. Rando (1984, 1988) addressed 29 separate categories acting simultaneously to affect the grief process.

Rando divides these categories into three main groupings: psychological factors, social factors, and physical factors. It is recommended that in order to understand the individuality of each griever, the mental health professional be familiar with each variable.

The assessment screening intake form used by HSGP is based on the variables presented by Rando adapted for use with homicide survivors. The death in homicide cases is sudden and unexpected with no anticipatory planning.

This synopsis explains each category in the HSGP intake form (see Appendix A).

Age of Survivor: Age reveals the state of chronological development of the griever in the family life cycle. Carter and McGoldrick (1980) explain that in each category of the family life cycle there are age-related goals and developmental tasks which must be achieved in order to maintain healthy functioning. Our society views the young adult and those in middle age as more capable of withstanding the blow of psychological trauma. This is not always the case since a griever may become *stuck* in attaining life goals at any age due to severe psychological trauma.

Age of Victim: The helplessness of a young child, adolescent, or elder often leads one to view that murder in those age categories as a greater traumatic incident. The young person was robbed of reaching one's potential and achievement of life's goals. The elderly person who may have achieved life's goals and be near the end of life was robbed of the dignity of a peaceful death. The age of the victim impacts the griever in all developmental life cycles.

Relationship to the Deceased: This reveals what degree of emotional attachment was present and subsequently severed. Survivors frequently say, "He was not just my brother, he was my idol, really my one and only friend." This behavior is discussed further under the sections on group membership and meaning of the loss in this chapter.

Circumstances of the Death: This is a most critical factor in the death. It includes location, time, place, type of weapon used, preceding events, how the griever was informed, who else was present, and the description of the shock and numbness experienced. It also relates to the viewing of the body of the deceased, the funeral or memorial, and how the griever has coped with the experiences of sadness, anger, guilt, and emotional turbulence. The severity of physical damage to the body of the victim may be critical. It appears the greater the degree of mutilation of the victim's body, the more severe the psychological damage to survivors.

Status of the Defendant: It is important for the survivor to know if the murderer has been apprehended and incarcerated. Those who know the defendant is locked away may still be suspicious but express feelings that some sense of justice has been rendered. This is unlike those whose cases are still unsolved who may live with paranoia, fear, and vulnerability regarding the fact that the defendant is still free to murder them, another loved one, or other innocent persons, which creates constant anxiety.

Court Experiences: When the case was resolved in court proceedings where the griever was present, the survivor appears to feel more knowledgeable about the occurrences, and more capable in addressing the grief work to be accomplished. Those who were kept out of court, either by the defense in order to enhance the case for the defendant, or by well-intentioned friends to *protect* the survivor appear to resent the intrusion, helplessness, and subsequent dependency. They chastise themselves for not having been able to withstand decisions which were made for them by others. Those whose case was *swept under the carpet* and never went to trial appear most overwhelmed with the sense of injustice.

Secondary Victimization Experiences: The importance of this variable necessitates a comprehensive analysis which was discussed in Chapter Three under complications, and is addressed in greater detail later in this chapter.

Roles and Functioning of the Deceased: The death of one's child at any age appears to provoke the most severe intense grief reaction. The loss is compounded for those whose deceased loved one functioned in multiple roles or a dominant decision-making role in the family system. Survivors may speak of loss of their confidant, advisor, lover, friend and other important emotionally attached roles. Revealing how the deceased functioned provides clues to the level of dependency in the relationship. Who will fill the position and achieve the necessary tasks previously accomplished by the deceased?

Roles and Function of Survivor Prior to Death: This indicates interdependence in the loss relationship. How dependent was the griever on the relationship for mutual emotional support? What skills must now be developed due to the death? A wife may need to develop skills to earn a living, manage money, become a single parent. A husband may need to develop skills to interrelate with school authorities, manage a household, and other necessary parenting functions.

Present Role and Functioning of Survivor: What is occurring now that brings the survivor to seek help? Survivors often are emotionally overwrought, with inability to eat, or sleep without nightmares. They report their confusion, inability to concentrate, becoming disorganized at work, irritability, and inability to control or understand their anger. They may have begun substance abuse to assist in coping, yet be fearful of long-term consequences of drug usage. Most report inability to control the intrusion of thoughts of the victim and murder scene, and murderous impulses. There is a sense of apprehension about the future and experience of multiple flashbacks.

Meaning of the Loss: The death may be grieved in multiple dimensions. A widow lost her job as a police officer following the shooting death of her husband by a hold-up gang at a convenience store. The police department determined she could no longer serve in the high stress area of law enforcement due to the symptoms she experienced following her husband's death. She said, "I lost my husband, the role of wife, and the role of police officer in one short moment." Explore the special qualities in the relationship and recognize how the person had a unique meaning in the life of the griever. Explore the secondary losses.

Relationship with Deceased: When the relationship was satisfying, warm, comforting, and supportive, the griever experiences a less severe grief reaction than if the relationship was fraught with conflict and ambivalence. Unresolved issues in a conflictual relationship are not ended by death and may present a more severe grief reaction.

Previous Crisis Experience: Few survivors present a history of previous crises that compare to the magnitude of the murder of a loved one. However, those who have experienced other deaths, illnesses in the family, other criminal victimization, natural disasters, or other crises experiences have developed coping mechanisms to support them through the event. There is some knowledge about what occurs physically, emotionally, and socially. Uncertainty and lack of knowledge breeds anxiety. And, in turn, anxiety paralyzes coping mechanisms. If the first crisis in life is the murder of a loved family member, the griever may be overwhelmed with the strangeness of the reactions. If multiple crises have occurred in the recent past, the griever may be even more impacted with the psychological assault.

Coping Mechanisms: A sample list of coping skills reveals how the griever has learned to cope. This provides an opportunity to explore what has been effective and ineffective in the past.

There are three distinct classifications: those who have had previous experience with crisis and who have developed positive coping skills, those with experience who developed negative coping skills, and those with no previous experience with fewer developed and identified coping mechanisms.

Previous Mental Health History: The survivor who is emotionally unstable at the time of the murder with a previous history of psychiatric difficulties will have a more difficult time resolving the loss. Pre-existing problems of emotional illness cannot be ignored. Those who suffer from depressive illness or borderline personality disorder should be excluded from group grief therapy and be seen for individual psychotherapy. Grief therapy is not the treatment of choice for these clients.

Present Health: An assessment of physical and emotional health characteristics indicates the ability of the griever to complete the arduous tasks of group grief work. Suicidal ideation is presented by most homicide survivors. The intent to rid one's self of the terrible pain by ending one's life is real and must be taken seriously. Employ the use of a written contract. The client writes out the contract with the promise no suicidal behavior will be acted on without notification and contact with the therapist. In addition, provide an immediate identified support network.

For those who present physical symptoms of stress, e.g., elevated blood pressure, colitis, migraine headaches, a physical examination by a physician is recommended. All clients admitted to individual therapy are requested to obtain a physical examination.

Past Experience with Death: The griever who has had no previous experience with death, or has never experienced other critical losses has a more intense grief reaction. Orienting clues as to what to expect in a grief reaction is lacking. Survivors with previous death experiences report that the reactions to other deaths were *NOT* as severe. However, the previous experience may have assisted the griever in development of coping skills.

Other Losses: Other prior major losses must be assessed. The person who has suffered multiple major losses may exhibit unresolved grief from several incidents and experience a more intense reaction to the present situation.

Social, Cultural, Ethnic, and Religious Affiliation: There are social mores, ethnic and cultural variations in the expression of emotions. As therapists, we must be knowledgeable about the acceptable practices, values and teachings of the survivor whom we serve. The Greeks and Italians may be more expressive, and openly relate their sense of loss and feelings of grief. Members of other cultural groups are more reserved and may not display signs of deep emotional attachment. This is not indicative that the grief reaction is less or the loss relationship means less.

Those who have a strong religious faith may receive comfort from their beliefs and practices within the religious community. Others may feel abandoned by their religion due to a compounded loss of expectations and conflict with church teachings. The symptoms of internal conflict and cognitive dissonance appear more severe in those with strong religious faiths. Historically, homicide survivors with a strong religious affiliation appear to have more difficulty resolving the conflicts brought on by murder than those with weaker religious affiliation.

Availability and Use of Support Systems: One of the most important factors for survivors is the availability of a strong support system. A community of caring supportive others alleviates some of the stressful reactions presented by the psychological trauma. This is particularly necessary during court proceedings and other unfamiliar situations. On the other hand, survivors may withdraw from supportive others or not use those who offer help. One of the greatest strengths assessed in survivors is the ability to have reached out for assistance which is evident by their presence in the intake session.

The screening intake session is scheduled for two hours, but more time will be needed to gain all the necessary information. As the therapist directs the group therapy sessions with the survivors, knowledge of these variables will assist in providing guidance and direction.

The mental health professional may discover other variables, which are present with enough frequency, to include in the screening intake for utilization with subsequent treatment groups.

Continue to explore issues for comprehensive assessment of the survivor which present related treatment issues. A review of Post Traumatic Stress Disorder alerts the clinician to consider unresolved grief as indicative of PTSD in a long-term crisis reaction.

POST TRAUMATIC STRESS DISORDER

The Diagnostic and Statistical Manual of Mental Disorders, Third Edition, Revised (DSM-III-R) (1987) provides a diagnostic classification for the long-range effects of psychological trauma. When a person survives a catastrophic incident there may be residual trauma and stress reactions for years. Many persons who experience long-term stress reactions continue to function although possibly at a less than optimal level. Stress reactions are the *NORMAL* response to a traumatic event. Those who are unable to function at a normal range, or who are experiencing difficulties in one or more areas may be diagnosed as suffering from Post Traumatic Stress Disorder (PTSD). Due to the nature of the crisis and the possibility that grief reactions may have to be repressed and delayed due to demands placed on the survivors by the court system, the diagnosis of PTSD and Delayed Grief may be evident in survivors of homicide.

309.89 Post-traumatic Stress Disorder

A.   "The person has experienced an event that is outside the range of usual human experience and that would be markedly distressing to almost anyone, e.g., serious threat or harm to one's children, spouse, or other close relatives and friends; sudden destruction of one's home or community; or seeing another person who has recently been, or is being, seriously injured or killed as the result of an accident or physical violence.

B.   The traumatic event is persistently re-experienced in at least one of the following ways:

(1)   recurrent and intrusive distressing recollections of the event (in young children, repetitive play in which themes or aspects of the trauma are expressed)

(2)   recurrent distressing dreams of the event

(3)   sudden acting or feeling as if the traumatic event were recurring (includes a sense of reliving the experience, illusions, hallucinations, and dissociative [flashbacks] episodes, even those that occur upon awakening or when intoxicated)

(4)   intense psychological distress at exposure to events that symbolize or resemble an aspect of the traumatic event, including anniversaries of the trauma

C. Persistent avoidance of stimuli associated with the trauma or numbing of general responsiveness (not present before the trauma), as indicated by at least three of the following:

(1) efforts to avoid thoughts or feelings associated with the trauma

(2) efforts to avoid activities or situations that arouse recollection of the trauma

(3) inability to recall an important aspect of the trauma (psychogenic amnesia)

(4) markedly diminished interest in significant activities (in young children, loss of recently acquired developmental skills such as toilet training or language skills)

(5) feelings of detachment or estrangement from others

(6) restricted range of affect, e.g., unable to have loving feelings

(7) sense of a foreshortened future, e.g., does not expect to have a career, marriage, or children, or a long life

D. Persistent symptoms of increased arousal (not present before the trauma) as indicated by at least two of the following:

(1) difficulty falling or staying asleep

(2) irritability or outbursts of anger

(3) difficulty concentrating

(4) hypervigilance

(5) exaggerated startle response

(6) physiologic reactivity upon exposure to events that symbolize or resemble an aspect of the traumatic event (e.g., a woman who was raped in an elevator breaks out in a sweat when entering any elevator)

E. Duration of the disturbance (symptoms in B, C, and D) of at least one month.

Specify delayed onset if the onset of symptoms was at least six months after the trauma.''

Clinicians in training are required to assess each homicide survivor by the PTSD diagnostic criteria. Experienced therapists are benefited by the use of this descriptive means of assessment. Review and use are appropriate with all types of crises situations and for other crime victims. Homicide survivors may present symptomatic behaviors characteristic of PTSD up to five years following the murder of a loved one. This becomes a normal range of functioning for this distinct population. All homicide survivors with whom I have worked were assessed at intake with some characteristics of PTSD. Survivors present with a history of nightmares, flashbacks, fear of strangers, emotional withdrawal, eating and sleeping disturbances, constant intrusion of thought of the murder, case-related associations, irritability, angry outbursts, and avoidance of reminders. Relief of the symptomatic behavior may prevent a confirmed long-term diagnosis of PTSD. The symptomatic behaviors are alleviated through grief work and resolution of the grief process.

TRIGGER EVENTS

Many survivors may continue to re-experience crisis reactions over a considerable duration of time. Information provided by NOVA (1987) for Crisis Response Team workers suggests that crisis reactions are usually in response to "trigger" events. These events may elicit the aversive stimulus response associated with the traumatic event, which was first experienced at death notification. Trigger events may be different for different survivors but may include:

1. **Identification of the Assailant:** A 20-year-old was accompanied by her father to line ups for two years. She was a witness to the murder of her 12-year-old sister. When she identified the murderer she became physically ill, requiring hospitalization.

2. **Sensing:** Individual may see, hear, touch, smell or taste something similar to something that one was acutely aware of during the trauma. A young woman who had to identify her sister's body after a brutal murder lost 24 pounds of body weight. She could not eat because she could smell and taste the blood seen in her sister's mouth at the time of the identification.

3. **Anniversaries of the Event:** The date, time and hour of a crisis situation are imprinted in long-term memory. On these dates it is not unusual to observe as severe a reaction as experienced at the occurrence. Feelings of anxiety, fear and vulnerability predominate.

4. **Holidays, and Nodal Life Events in the Family:** Parents whose child has died report an overwhelming sadness at holidays, graduations and weddings of their friends' children many years later. If the crisis event occurred in close proximity to or on a holiday, this becomes an additional trigger.

5. **Hearings, Trials, Appeals and Other Criminal Justice Proceedings:** After a number of years, the lack of acknowledgment expressed about the victim as a real person creates additional stress. The criminal justice system is a chronic stressor.

6. **Media Articles About a Similar Event:** Articles may draw attention like a magnet even when the person knows there will be an adverse reaction. The mind continuously seeks to comprehend the meaning of the psychological trauma. Survivors may relate exact details and similarities from television shows to one's own family reactions.

SECONDARY VICTIMIZATION

As mental health professionals, we must become aware of the secondary assaults which the homicide survivor experiences. A secondary victimization can elicit a similar emotional reaction as that which occurs following the original criminal act. In some cases, a victim survivor can be even more traumatized by the second injury. The victim is in a state of emotional dependency, trusting that help will be provided, has established lifelong expectations of care by our systems, and is further shocked and frustrated at the lack of the systems' response to identified needs. The secondary victimization is committed by those the victim turns to for assistance.

NOVA (1987) notes sources of secondary victimization may include:

- The criminal justice system
- The media
- Family, friends, co-workers, employers, acquaintances
- Clergy
- Medical personnel
- Mental health professionals
- Social service workers
- Victim service workers
- School guidance counselors, teachers, educators
- Victim compensation system

Some secondary victimization from the criminal justice system can be prevented or alleviated by assurance that victim survivors are provided information in:

- Dealing with the media
- Criminal justice terminology
- Criminal justice procedures and proceedings
- How to receive notification when defendants are released on bail or bond
- Securing protection to reduce fear of retaliation
- Reasons for continuances
- Consultation and agreement to plea bargains
- Possibility of mistrial and not guilty verdict
- Need for Impact Statement, verbal testimony at sentencing
- Individual involvement in the criminal justice process
- The appellate process, possibility of conviction being overturned
- Parole hearings, parole, work-release programs and probation
- Availability of support programs

We must acknowledge the need to provide information at a level the particular family being provided services can understand. The impact of the secondary victimization or *assault* to a victim's emotional well being is intensified because of the duration of events and the numerous *assailants* associated with the criminal justice process.

Victimization by Outside Others

Outside of the criminal justice system, victim survivors may endure secondary victimization from other caretakers in the community to whom they turned for help.

> The mother of a child who was murdered went to her parish priest for comfort and solace. Instead, she was told to "forgive" the person who had killed her four-year-old daughter. It was not the comfort she sought nor expected, and not the support she needed. She did not need to deal with additional guilt because she could not "forgive" her child's murderer. Thus unable to obey the dictates of her priest, she withdrew from her church.

Family members and friends of victim survivors frequently add to the secondary victimization. This may occur out of concern for the survivor or from their own sense of helplessness and frustration seeing what their loved one must endure. Others may attempt to minimize the seriousness of the crime. They may tell the victim survivor to stop talking about "it"; suggest calling the murder "an accident"; insist the victim survivor "get on with life"; or attempt to play "one-upmanship" with their own horror stories. The survivor expecting support, understanding and compassion is forced to recognize that those closest to him, in fact, may not have the ability to help and may create additional pain and hardship.

> A 17-year-old high school girl's father was murdered by her stepmother. She did not know how to help her own mother. The kids at school made jokes about "killing your old man." She learned to joke, kid, and hide the pain. Ten years later, as a member of a HSGP grief therapy group she worked through her unresolved grief. This obviously was more difficult than if she could have done her grief work at the time of her father's death.

Those closest to the survivor may themselves be emotionally overwrought with grief. It is difficult to help loved ones when dealing with one's own frustration, anger, helplessness, shame, and other painful grief reactions. Individual family members, in an effort to deal with their shock and grief at the same time, may create additional trauma for one another.

> The mother of two young boys whose father was murdered spoke of her difficulties with the children. She was irritable, short-tempered and recognized that she was being over-protective out of fear for their safety. She said, "They can't understand why I keep having to take days off to go to court, and I can't ever take time off for them. They are acting like brats and I don't even want to be with them.

I don't know what to believe anymore, Bob was supposed to be our protector and he couldn't even protect himself. What am I supposed to teach the boys about being men?''

Preparation for Secondary Victimization

Mental health professionals and victim service providers can assist to prevent some secondary victimization through education and preparation. Suggestions include:

- Inform the victim survivor of services offered by your office. Be clear and concise. Avoid making promises you can not keep. Put directions and appointments in writing.

- Explain that not all family members and friends may be able to offer emotional support when it is most needed. Alert victim survivors to possibility of secondary victimization. Cite examples of how it occurs and explain the reasons for its occurrence.

- Offer a list of available support groups in your area. Make sure you are making an adequate referral. A victim survivor who is given a list of five agencies to contact and then finds no one to assist is being given false hopes and is further victimized.

- Develop a list of terms and definitions that the victims will frequently hear as the case progresses through the criminal justice process.

- Explain in detail criminal justice procedures, such as arraignment, pre-trial, trial, victim impact statements, sentencing guidelines, bond and bail, so the victim survivor has knowledge of what is happening presently and what may occur in the future.

The intensity, frequency, and duration of long-term stress reactions usually decreases over a period of time. The use of new coping mechanisms learned to deal with the crisis will influence all three factors. The person who is motivated to address the emotional trauma and work on one's personal grief reaction, and does so despite these complications, presents with higher levels of adaptive functioning. We have the opportunity not only to provide services and support to persons in crisis, but to teach new methods to help one cope with other problems in life. The psychological effects of a catastrophic trauma such as the murder of a loved one can be alleviated. There is no cure. The objective is to help the person *integrate* the trauma into the psyche so life can be continued within an acceptable functional range.

TREATMENT ISSUES

SCREENING INTAKE FORMAT

Provide a two-hour appointment session for intake of survivors. Each one of the group co-leaders in clinical training is required to take one-half of the client load, with the group leader attending all intakes. The longer session provides instruction time and review of the psychodynamics of each case between the leader and co-leaders, following the client's departure. The intake session may not be ample to cover all the necessary assessment but will provide a good basis on which to proceed in therapy. Survivors may reveal personal information at intake that will not be addressed in group sessions until perhaps much later in therapy, or may not be revealed to the group members at all. All information is confidential and must be acknowledged as such. The design of the intake form used by HSGP has been revised several times to meet the needs of the client and therapist (see Appendix A).

It is preferable to limit the intake to 12 clients per group. There will be a normal attrition rate of those who seek help but decide not to proceed in group therapy. There will be those for whom group treatment is not appropriate and will require individual therapy, and those who come to one or two group sessions and drop out. The ideal group size of eight members is more easily achieved with the scheduled intake of 12 clients.

Meeting with two group leaders for the screening intake serves to reduce the survivor's anxiety at the first group meeting. The survivor has a base of familiarity with more than one therapist.

Survivors are informed they will be telephoned about admission to the treatment program as soon as possible. When the client is not appropriate for the group treatment program, they are informed of the recommended treatment at time of intake.

As was previously noted, group treatment may not be the treatment of choice for some survivors. This will be revealed in a comprehensive assessment of the client.

> A nurse who worked on a psychiatric unit was required to attend some type of community group as part of her work-related skills development. Her son had been killed by the police and a week later her estranged husband committed suicide. The circumstances indicated she would be appropriate for the group until she informed the co-leaders she would not be able to do any of the work. She just wanted assurances her presence would be documented for her employer. She had been previously seen in individual therapy and had a history of missing scheduled appointments. She had been seen in emergency visits during three other crisis. She was deemed inappropriate due to her stated lack of motivation, and the previous individual therapy experience.
>
> Others who are inappropriate for group treatment are: hospitalized schizophrenic patients, and those who present borderline personality disorders.

Tasks of Grief Work

William Worden (1982) defined four tasks of grief work. They are: 1) To accept the reality of the loss, 2) Experience the pain of loss, 3) Adjust to an environment where the deceased is missing, and, 4) Withdrawal of emotional energy from the deceased and re-investment into other relationships. The group treatment program is designed to guide the survivor through these tasks of grief work. This is a painful process. The group members are assessed for their own capability to withstand the arduous task of reliving, reviewing, and confronting unpleasant feelings. A support system is identified at the time of intake. Members are encouraged to alert their family or other supportive members to understand the trauma they will be experiencing as they go through the grief work in the group treatment program. Some survivors are unable to share the experience, have no one to talk to and are chastised by family members to "just let it go." Those who have family support appear to make better progress than those without the supportive understanding of outside others.

USE OF GENOGRAM

The genogram is a three-generational diagram of all persons living and deceased in the family system. Used as an assessment tool, it provides the clinician the opportunity to examine the history and patterns of the family. The genogram may be sketched during intake: recording names, dates of death, marriage, divorce, moves, or other life events. The genogram serves to identify all the members of the family, sibling positions, roles and functions of members, conflictual relationships and emotionally cut-off members. This tool helps to define family patterns, rigid or flexible rules, lines of communication, and the availability of a support system for the survivor. Oftentimes, the genogram reveals to survivors sources of support which would not have been thought of as available. A history of previous psychological trauma is easily noted with this assessment guide.

In the group treatment program, members are provided a copy of their individual family genogram after several sessions. It is a working document helping survivors recognize patterns which they have established, providing direction in opening communication lines to other family members, and helping in understanding the response to this psychological trauma and to other crisis in their lives.

For the therapist, the genogram provides an overview of the family system and immediate identification of any secondary problem areas.

McGoldrick and Gerson (1985) have provided an excellent guide on genograms for family assessment. Similar to adding information for the intake session, additional genogram information may be added after each group session.

GROUP MEMBERSHIP

Relationship issues may be considered in the selection of group members. Relationship configurations in a family are variable. The nuclear family system consists of the parents, spouses, children and sibling relationships. The extended family includes grandparents, aunts, uncles, in-laws, cousins, and other associated relationships. A relationship with a live-in partner may be as emotionally close and dependent as one where the spouses have been married for years. Survivors may have an emotional attachment to an aunt or grandmother as close as that in a parental relationship. Equally, a close friendship with a girl or boy friend who has been murdered will reveal emotional dynamics similar to that of family relationships.

In the HSGP program we do not establish treatment groups according to relationship to the victim. Nor do we deny access to the treatment program for lack of being a socially accepted family member. A mother, father, child, aunt, grandfather, lover, spouse, friend or sibling may be included in one group. However, they are all survivors of different murder victims. It is preferable not to have members of one family attend the same group treatment program. Each person's relationship with the victim is unique. One of the tasks of group grief therapy is to examine those relationships in detail. It is important that the survivor feel free to discuss issues openly which, if another family member were present, might not be revealed or dealt with. In a highly anxious system family secrets surface and may be part of issues that can only be resolved within a group of strangers.

In this context, each member has the opportunity to learn how members of other families are reacting to the victimization. A 50-year-old mother will learn what helped a 32-year-old surviving sibling in her group, and transfer this knowledge to her own surviving children. A wife will learn from another's husband how to relate to her own spouse. Children learn what their own parents may be experiencing as they listen to the anguish of other parents.

LENGTH OF TIME AFTER MURDER

We have had the experience in HSGP of admitting survivors to the group therapy program too soon after the murder. If survivors are still in shock and experiencing psychic numbness from the trauma, they are unable to relate or recognize the emotional process. These clients *CANNOT* complete assignments, do not recognize the value of the work, and are in effect, in "frozen fright" and inappropriate for group at that time.

The early admission survivor may come to every session, attend with quiet attention, resist confrontation with denial, and complete the treatment program but never do any grief work. Later, when it would be more appropriate for attendance, the client has already tried group, and it didn't work! *DO NOT ADMIT TOO SOON!*

The ideal time for admission to the group appears to be in the four-to-six-month period following the murder. This is the time of greatest disorganization and disorientation. Each survivor must be assessed individually. A clear sense of the variables the griever is dealing with in the grieving process is more important than the passage of time since the murder. Most of the HSGP clients are admitted into the treatment program within the first year up to 15 years after the murder.

For the majority, the long delay was due to the lack of an available treatment program and a waiting list of 62 survivors when the pilot program was started. The ideal time for admission has been documented as within the first year. A support network of trained volunteers are required to assist the newly bereaved the first two to five months; followed by group therapy; then joining the mutual peer support group and maintaining that support system throughout the trial period.

INFORMATION SHEET

After the pilot program, we found it helpful to provide written information for new group members. The HSGP survivors receive a printed sheet with the following information upon acceptance into the program. Included is the address, directions, date and time of the assigned group.

"Grief Therapy is emotionally draining and will require a great amount of energy. Please ask your family and friends to be aware of your need for support, particularly for the first six to eight sessions.

You may feel and express anger of which you were unaware previously, or have not recognized in this intensity. *DO NOT LET THIS FRIGHTEN YOU!* Your expressions of anger will assist others to see their anger as normal and each will be able to express himself more openly. If you are angry with another member, it is your insight and comment which may be most helpful. We are here to help one another in the resolution of grief, not *protect,* but *"RESOLVE."* Be open and honest with yourself and others.

If you feel anger and do not express it, you may feel guilty, e.g., 'How could I be angry at that poor woman with all she has suffered?' *UNEXPRESSED ANGER LEADS TO GUILT!* Anger is one of your most therapeutic weapons. Let the group help you to work through it and discharge it safely and appropriately.

Homework assignments may be difficult to accomplish. Do the best you can, no one will ask for more. It is your grief and it is as unique as your fingerprints. Grief therapy will be most effective for those who are able to complete the assignments.

In some sessions you may feel unable to share your thinking or feelings. Your commitment to attend all 12 sessions is important. Attend the session even if you do not verbally share. *YOUR PRESENCE AND SUPPORT IS NEEDED BY ALL MEMBERS."*

Telephone numbers of available therapists are listed below the above information. Arrangements are made that one therapist will be available at all hours for telephone support counseling between sessions. Survivors are assured that a therapist will be available.

GRIEF EXPERIENCE INVENTORY

Therapists have volumes of information on grief symptoms and behavioral characteristics which indicate the survivor is experiencing an acute, complicated, delayed, or exaggerated grief reaction. However, most, if not all, the information is subjective. It is difficult to measure the intensity, frequency, or duration of bereavement symptoms considering the multiple impinging variables without an objective test instrument. For the HSGP Treatment Program the Grief Experience Inventory (GEI) test instrument was chosen as an evaluative method to determine progress for each survivor using objective criteria.

The GEI was developed in a five year research study by Catherine M. Sanders, Paul A. Mauger, and Paschal N. Strong, Jr., at the University of South Florida in Tampa in 1979. The GEI was developed to meet the need for an objective, multidimensional measure of grief.

The GEI is composed of 135 true-false statements. It provides measurement for nine grief characteristics: despair, anger, guilt, social isolation, loss of control, rumination, depersonalization, somatization, and death anxiety. The test provides validity scales measuring denial, atypical responses, and social desirability. The test is easily administered to the group; the pre-test in the first session and the post-test in the final session.

Results for those tested in the HSGP Treatment Program are presented in Chapter Six in the evaluative section following the final session of grief therapy. Unfortunately, the pilot program group members were not provided this testing. Use of the GEI instrument or another with which you are familiar is recommended for all group programs.

RELEASE FORM INFORMATION

The HSGP group sessions have been audiotaped and filmed by use of videotape recordings. This has been done as a basis for utilization in training other psychotherapists. Homicide survivors are requested to sign a release form at time of intake. All survivors have expressed their willingness to share this work in order that others may be helped throughout the country. (see Appendix B).

The VCR recordings and audiotaping are reviewed with the group co-leaders at the mid-evaluation and final evaluation training sessions. This provides therapists an opportunity to enhance their skills, to acknowledge areas which need improvement, and to visually measure behavioral progress of the group members.

FEE STRUCTURE

The HSGP pilot program was designed to charge group members no more than an minimal amount for the 12-week Group Grief Therapy Treatment Program. There is a therapeutic value in charging some fee for service, but the fee was set low enough for participation by most survivors. Those who are unable to pay have been provided free service. Insurance is utilized by those clients who have appropriate coverage. Thirty percent of HSGP clients have been unable to pay and their fees are covered by contributions from the community. Survivors who have completed therapy have formed a core of volunteers who plan and administer fund-raising events. These funds go directly to the cost of providing therapy for those unable to pay.

THERAPEUTIC TECHNIQUES

Prior to beginning the group treatment program, it will be helpful to review some of the therapeutic techniques useful in the group process.

- **Use of Death Words:** Use the words *murder, killed, died;* licenses *expire,* there are many types of *crises* and *tragedies;* the actual descriptive words help the survivor face the reality of the death. It is not hidden behind euphemisms.

- **Use the Proper Name of the Murder Victim:** not the *body* or other pronouns (it, him, her, them), the deceased person is a *Very Important Person* in the life of the survivor.

- **Cleanup of Site:** The cleanup of a home where a loved one has been murdered may present trigger events for an indeterminate length of time. The cleanup is difficult for family members and friends and is best accomplished by those who provide cleaning services. Session 9 in Chapter Six addresses additional issues the cleanup presents.

- **Viewing of Body:** Encourage viewing to confirm the reality of death whenever possible. See Session 9, Chapter Six.

- **Release of Anger and Guilt:** Lifton (1979) describes the use of confrontation, reordering and renewal in providing a framework for this cognitive restructuring.

  A. Confrontation: The therapist asks questions which encourages verbalization. The client relates events as they were, using imagery to recall details, and recognizing threat to self. The client recognizes that they no longer are the same or in that position. Written assignments will bring flooding of emotions and thoughts which are then confronted.

  B. Reordering: This may be achieved through writing, reporting, exploration of guilt, anger, blame, stigma, shame, fear, vulnerability. Examine what was done, and not done. Survivors are asked, what could have been done, what they wish had been done, and what can be done now? An active struggle with guilt associated thoughts takes place. Example: a father who purchased a gun after his daughter's murder reordered his thinking when he recognized: 1) he could not have protected his daughter if he had owned a gun at the time of her murder; 2) he could not kill a human being; 3) he detested the use of violence; 4) he was a mild mannered, quiet man; and, 5) his actions and thoughts were in conflict with his value and belief system. After this reordering process, he sold the gun and reported feeling more secure. He had been trying to cope in a manner that was foreign and unacceptable for him.

  C. Renewal: A sense of renewal takes place with reviving and reviewing thoughts of life as it was, there is a replaying of the scenario in the imagery. The client finds recognition that one did one's best, accepting one's inactivation under the circumstances of the murder with an ability to forgive oneself. The ability to say good-bye, make decisions, and offer assistance to others is evident. This begins an active effort to make things better for self and others.

- **Active Listening Skills:** Listen with the *third ear.* Listen to the words used, the non-verbal messages, and explore the feelings which may not be verbalized. Recognize secondary losses and secondary victimization.

- **Open Communications Within the Family:** Encourage members who are fearful and withdrawn to talk to family members and teach them the value of not burying their anger and guilt. Explain that it is not protective to keep secrets but adds to the anxiety in each member.

- **Teach Normal Grief Symptoms:** There is a reduction of fear and anxiety as one learns the reaction is normal for the experience of the abnormal event.

- **Encourage Attendance at Hearings, Trials and All Court Proceedings:** The survivor needs knowledge and affirmation that the victim and survivors are important to society.

Attendance renews a sense of control and relieves guilt through the *representation of the loved one.* The courts, prosecution and defense, must be made to recognize this murder is not just another statistic but a tragic time in the lives of human beings.

- **Legitimize Responses:** Whatever the survivor expresses in terms of murderous impulses, anger, rage, guilt, shame, stigma, blame or other symptomatic responses are to be acknowledged as within a normal range of expected behaviors. The intensity, frequency and duration will be lessened by ventilation and validation.

- **Prepare Survivors for Behavioral and Cognitive Reactions of Stress:** Explain that survivors may have difficulty sleeping, experience reduced appetite, exhibit decreased sexual desire, or that the converse may occur. Explain that this is one's individual reaction and the body responds in its most natural adaptive manner.

- **Explain Disconnected, Intrusive and Disorganized Thinking:** Reassure that this is *NORMAL.* Suggest the survivor make a written notation on a small pad of the thought when it intrudes while at work or during other activity. Then, it will not be forgotten. It is given the status it deserves, and can be addressed later in the day in written assignments. A HSGP group member reported that her 80 year old grandmother had been instructed to wear a rubber band around her wrist to be snapped at the intrusive thoughts of her son's murder. *DO NOT SUGGEST A RUBBER BAND AROUND THE WRIST TO BE SNAPPED AT INTRUSIVE THOUGHTS!* This is an insult and discounts the survivors thinking as unimportant. The thought is important but must be addressed later. Only when the thought has been thoroughly reviewed will it begin to recede.

- **Remember the ART OF SILENCE:** This is particularly evident preceding a major breakthrough for a survivor as one struggles to put into words one's most inner thoughts and feelings.

- **Respect the Uniqueness of Grief:** Each survivor struggles in his own individual way to cope with major psychological trauma.

Those who have taken the path to make the crisis an opportunity, often prefer the more understanding, sadder but wiser person they have become. They would trade everything they *had to learn,* to have life as it once was, but the events cannot be changed. All that can be changed is one's ability to cope and this can be achieved for the majority of survivors through focused grief therapy.

The next two chapters take the therapist step-by-step through each session of the Group Grief Therapy Treatment Program. It will be helpful to review the previous session each week prior to meeting with the group. This is a guide. It has been proven workable and therapeutic. It is a challenge to reach out to help those who need guidance, support and knowledge.

*"If one is to survive the losses suffered in a tragic crisis,
he must hold up the image of what was, reviewing in detail,
reviving memories of what life had been. Only then, can he
begin to accept the change and begin the process of resolution."*
Gerald Caplan

CHAPTER FIVE

Group Grief Therapy Treatment Program Sessions 1-6

The next two chapters outline the 12-week Group Grief Therapy Treatment Program. Each chapter is divided into six sessions. This provides for the use of a mid-group evaluative instrument and mid-group case reports from the supervisory session with the medical director.

All cases are true with names changed to protect the anonymity of the survivors. Permission has been granted by the clients in order to share this learning experience.

A check-off list of preparations includes:

1. Provide the Required Reading List and Self-Awareness exercise assignments to group co-leader therapists one month before group is to begin.

2. Obtain the Grief Experience Inventory evaluative instrument.

3. Prepare copies of materials to be handed out for each session.

4. Obtain signed consent on release form at time of intake.

5. Provide clients verbal and written directions to the group meeting site.

6. Review intake form on each client with co-leaders prior to Session I.

7. Review the completed Self-Awareness assignment with each co-leader prior to Session I.

8. Complete other tasks as required for individual program.

Prior to beginning the Group Grief Therapy Treatment Program, an overview of the objectives will be helpful. This is intended to provide a roadmap so that the direction and progress can be measured and, thereby, more easily attained.

GOALS AND OBJECTIVES

Worden (1982) outlined four tasks of mourning. Harper (1987) arranged the tasks into the acronym, "TEAR," which helps the clinician remember and gage the activity of grief work as the mourner works through the grief process. The Grief Therapy Treatment Program, although not originally designed with the tasks in mind, correlates with the tasks throughout the twelve sessions. Using the word TEAR, note how the process follows in the twelve sessions of group therapy. The four tasks are defined goals to achieve in the therapeutic environment of the group.

T - To Accept The Reality Of The Loss
This is to come to term with the reality that the person is dead and will not return. Accepting the permanence and irreversibility of death is primary.

Sessions I, II, III: This is achieved as the griever reviews through the mental rehearsal of events. Each time the story is told, denial is lessened. The review of who the person was, what one could have become, and examination of what the loss means is necessary.

E - Experience The Pain Of Loss
This is to not avoid or suppress the pain, but to feel the loss as the painful void in life that it is; to work through the pain. To be able to express the physical, emotional, social, and behavioral pain without apology or denial.

Sessions IV, V, VI: A safe non-judgmental environment is provided to express thoughts, feelings, and behavior without fear of recourse. Expressions of anger, guilt, shame, stigma, fear, and vulnerability are revealed. There are examinations of *unfinished business,* ambivalence, identification with the deceased, and exploration of family relationships. There are confrontations of difficult issues in family systems.

A - Adjust To Environment Where Deceased Is Missing
The griever adjusts through decision making, defining goals, and planning for a future without the deceased. The survivor experiences the changes in the home, work, and social environment due to the death. New roles and learning skills must be developed to function in unfamiliar, new life roles.

Sessions VII, VIII, IX: These sessions provide examination of roles and functional positions of family members; opening communications in closed systems, secret keeping; rebuilding relationships; then review of the funeral to bring back into focus the finality. There will be relief of guilt, anxiety, and fear, and cognitive restructuring of life events.

R - Reinvestment of Life Into Other Relationships and Withdrawal of Emotional Energy From Deceased

This is the most difficult of tasks unless the mourner accepts that the deceased is not dishonored by the investment of the mourner's life energies into new relationships. The mourner may not reinvest because the pain of loss was so great, one cannot risk another painful loss. Grievers may reinvest into work goals or changes to make the world a better place for others.

Sessions X, XI, XII: The memorial service honors the dead with a living memory among the group members, review of new fears, and plans for future-oriented growth and development. Evaluations reveal where one was, what one hoped to achieve, what one has achieved and learned about oneself in the process. One of the measures of resolution is the ability to speak of the dead without tearing or experiencing the deep painful feelings of loss.

Mourning may last for years. It seldom is resolved under two years and the complications with which the bereaved homicide survivor must deal may revive grief symptoms until the criminal justice system closes the litigation. Grief therapy serves to mitigate the deep painful sorrow, and assist the survivor to continue in life at a higher functional level than the survivor believed to be possible in the face of such overwhelming psychological trauma.

The objectives for each session, tasks required to achieve and maintain a therapeutic group process, homework assignments for group members, and assignments for group co-leaders in training are outlined. This is followed by the rationale for the process and the materials selected for the session. Study questions at the end of each session are required as written homework assignments for group co-leaders in clinical training.

Session One

INTRODUCTIONS

OBJECTIVES

1. Introduction of group members at level that appears most comfortable for each individual member.

2. Identification of group norms, goals, and individual expectations.

3. Provision of Grief Experience Inventory pre-test.

4. Normalization of the symptoms of the grief process.

5. Enhancement of member's recognition of similarities and differences in experiences as family members of homicide victims.

GROUP PROCESS

1. Provide setting conducive to open interchange; chairs arranged so each participant can visually see one another without obstruction.

2. Explain use of audiotaping and VCR filming, and obtain any signed consents not previously obtained during initial screening intake. Establish confidentiality of materials and of all group participation.

3. Introduce self, co-leaders; identify own interest and concern in working with survivors of homicide.

4. Provide a telephone number of at least one therapist who will be available for telephone counseling for the group members between sessions. Make arrangements that one therapist will always be available for telephone contact!

5. Request a commitment for regular attendance for the twelve-week sessions; encourage participation. Accept individual members to volunteer in assigned roles to make coffee, collect donations, duplicate materials, assist in audiotaping, and select an acting librarian.

6. Provide at least 30 minutes to administer Grief Experience Inventory test instrument.

7. Request that each member introduce himself to the group, relating as much information as his comfort level permits.

8. Explain use of Grief Book; give homework assignments; provide first session handout: Grief Symptomatology (Redmond, 1979).

HOMEWORK ASSIGNMENT FOR SURVIVORS

1. Write out your personal objectives for joining the group at this time.

ASSIGNMENT FOR THERAPISTS IN TRAINING

1. Write out professional objectives for your training.

2. Write out objectives for the group as therapist co-leaders.

3. Read: Bowen (1976) in P. Guerin, (ed.), *Family Therapy, Theory and Practice,* "Family Reaction to Death."

4. Write out study questions.

RATIONALE

It is important to provide a comfortable setting conducive to group interaction. The group members will attend the first session with a high level of anxiety. Most survivors never have had a previous experience in therapy or even met a psychotherapist or grief therapist. They may be unsure of what to expect from the group or the therapist.

As the therapists introduce themselves they may provide role modeling by taking risks to share their own experiences, interests, and concerns for the group.

The introduction of individual members and the description of the murder will probably not reveal the depth or range of emotions assessed in the individual screening intake session. It is important to remember it takes time to build trust. The sharing of deep personal grief is a risk to each individual because there is the fear of lack of acknowledgment and understanding predicted by previous actual experience with others.

As the members develop trust in one another and the co- leaders, each will share at one's own comfort level. Members may closely identify with one another due to the circumstances of the situations, but must be provided time to reveal the depth of pain of this loss openly to this group of strangers. Non-judgmental acceptance of the information revealed will be instrumental in providing a transference.

The Grief Experience Inventory (GEI) pre-test is administered in the first session to establish a baseline measurement for later determination of the progress made in the treatment program. The GEI post-test will be administered in the final session.

Books are provided to be checked out to each participant on a weekly basis. The titles chosen are generally those written by laypersons and professionals who have experienced a death and were expressive in working through the grief process through their writings. Titles are listed in the References as Suggested Reading.

Lattanzi (1984), Grollman (1981), and Conner (1987), have suggested that bibliotherapy and grief writing are excellent as therapeutic techniques in grief therapy.

The requirement of written objectives will assist the survivor to focus on present circumstances, assess what changes need to be pursued, and give the member a beginning sense of control. This self-awareness is conducive to cutting through some of the confusion. By listing the expectations and objectives, each individual provides himself with a tool for measurement of progress.

In order to normalize grief reactions experienced, the first handout of Grief Symptomatology is provided. A sense of control increases as the griever gains knowledge about the grief process. Each can identify one's own personal reactions and experiences as *not crazy,* but within the range of normal symptoms.

Therapists are requested to identify objectives as a measurement tool for professional and group goals. The reading assignment provides an overview of the family system as it responds to the death of one of its members.

STUDY QUESTIONS

1.   In what ways might the "emotional shockwave" as described by Bowen manifest itself in family members of a murder victim?

2.   What grief reactions might be expressed by an emotionally cutoff member?

3.   In what ways does the functional level of the deceased and the dependency level of the survivor affect the grief process?

4.   Compare this experience in the initial session with homicide survivors to groups of survivors from other causes of death. How do these differ? What similarities are apparent? What preparation would assist the therapist to work with this client population?

Session Two

GRIEF AND MOURNING

OBJECTIVES

1. To acknowledge and meet the needs and objectives of group members.

2. To provide a supportive atmosphere in which members feel secure to express themselves.

3. To normalize grief reactions which have been identified and expressed.

GROUP PROCESS

1. Ask members to share written objectives from homework assignment. Discuss expectations of each at individual's own comfort level.

2. Summarize those expressed and insure that individual issues will be addressed, e.g., one member experiencing nightmares with inability to sleep; another with issues of non-supportive family members.

3. Address grief reactions that have surfaced during week in response to grief therapy.

4. Explore issue of other family member's responses to survivor attending the therapy group.

5. Identify supportive network within member's family system.

6. Provide reading material: Knapp (1986), *Beyond Endurance When A Child Dies,* "The Family and Bereavement, Course of Adjustment, Parental Response to the Murder of a Child."

HOMEWORK ASSIGNMENT

1. Write out a personal description of the deceased. Write of capabilities, lifestyle, values, beliefs, personality, personal appearance, activities, opinions, how he thought and felt about issues; anything the survivors can remember as indicative of *who has died?*

2. Identify what roles the deceased fulfilled in the family system. Who has taken on the functional tasks of each role? Has this changed daily activities and the expectations of others due to role reversal or conflict?

ASSIGNMENT FOR THERAPIST

1.   Write out normal grief reactions and symptomatology of survivors.

2.   Contrast and compare symptoms presented by survivors of homicide with identified normal symptoms.

3.   Read: Wass, H. (1979) ed., *Dying, Facing The Facts,* Jackson, "Bereavement and Grief," p. 256-281; Davidson, "Mourning Process Not Understood," p. 173-180.

RATIONALE

Group members will recognize individual expectations as similar to other members. Some issues will surface that others felt *alone* in experiencing or expressing. This normalizes the experience and provides identification and cohesion in the group. With objectives identified, the therapist has the opportunity to guide the group to meet individual needs. Flexibility must be allowed to work the defined goals into the group process.

A review of normal grief reactions will continue to lessen the psychological trauma of the unknown and identify unfamiliar reactions experienced by survivors since the murder.

Group members will experience a deepened sadness, depression, and psychic pain during grief therapy. They need to be prepared for this re-awakening of fresh psychic pain which may be similar to the first reactions to the death. The family support system is identified so that each may share the expected depressive reactions. Family members who have been alerted to expect the reactions have the opportunity to be more supportive. Encouraging the survivor to share openly some of the painful feelings within one's own family system further opens communication within the family. Group members may help one another identify who in the family may be supportive or suggest how to ask for support, e.g., "What worked for me . . ."

The handout by Knapp (1986) provides further insight into how grief of homicide survivors differs from grief due to other deaths. The graph reveals despair as a normal component and shows disorganization over a longer time period. However, recovery does eventually occur. This helps in providing a sense of hope to the survivors.

The assignment to write out a description of the deceased is intended to begin the process of differentiation from the deceased. This review also helps the griever in the process of decathexis. This, an internalized adaptation of a new relationship with the deceased established on memories of what was, and will never be again, is necessary in order to begin to form a new identity without the lost loved one. Rando (1984) reaffirms that the thoughts, feelings, memories and expectations that bind the griever to the deceased must be revived, reviewed, reexperienced and released.

The act of writing a description, thinking through who the deceased was, what he valued, his beliefs, his behaviors, his personality as perceived by the survivor, may bring a flooding of emotion to the surface. This may sharply focus the reality of the loss because there is recognition that the writing is based on memories and not on physical presence. Searching and yearning behaviors may be apparent and described. For those who are unable to write more than a few descriptive words, the therapists must be supportive, understanding, and patiently encourage without rushing the process.

Examination and exploration of roles will begin to help the griever acknowledge there are changes brought about due to the death that are unrelated to the murder. So much energy goes into the act of how the loved one was killed, it becomes difficult at best to acknowledge the significance within the family system. Role conflicts may be experienced as the adaptive spouse suddenly finds new skills must be developed and roles must be taken which were never necessary before. Role reversal also may be experienced, as a child must begin to care for a parent.

> Sally, 30, the youngest of three siblings was suicidal on intake into the group. She had enjoyed a strong, positive, personal relationship with every member of her family prior to the murder of her father three years previously. She resented everyone calling upon her for advice after the murder in Ohio. She had taken on the tasks of funeral arrangements, met with attorneys, and helped clean out the family home. She then flew back to complete her wedding plans, enter a new marriage, and establish her home in Florida. She was so grief stricken, that the first two years after the murder were a nightmare.
>
> There were constant complaints from her grandmother, uncle, brother and sister about what happened to cherished photos, prize antiques, Dad's jewelry and other complaints about the estate settlement. Sally gave birth to a daughter the week of the trial held in Ohio. Her siblings and other relatives could not attend the legal proceedings even though they lived close by. She found herself in a decision-making role with her mother and grandmother. Sally expressed it, "I lost my whole family when Dad was murdered!"
>
> When asked about the roles in which her father had functioned, and who had replaced him, she was shocked to see how she had proceeded into the dominant role of father who always had cared for the others. Seldom did anyone agree with his decisions, but the family system had replaced him with a new "black sheep."

The assignment for therapists provides a recognition of normal grief patterns as outlined by major authorities in the field of thanatology. The comparative analysis of works by Rando (1984), Sanders (1984), Bowlby and Parkes (1970), and Worden (1982), were chosen to reveal how various clinicians have conceptualized the mourning process. This is intended to broaden the therapist's knowledge base, and alert one to observations of relevant phenomena seen in grievers during therapy.

The study question to review the process of introjection and identification helps the clinician to recognize the intrapsychic processes which grievers are working through in the process of mourning.

STUDY QUESTIONS

1. Compare and contrast Rando's grief assessment; Sander's "Bereavement Typologies and Implications for Therapy"; Bowlby and Parkes descriptions of the mourning process.

2. Write out Worden's "four tasks of mourning," and what the griever experiences during each task. What therapeutic interventions might be helpful throughout the process? What might indicate the survivor is unable to complete each task?

3. Write out definitions for the intrapsychic processes of introjection and identification.

Session Three

RELATIONSHIP WITH DECEASED

OBJECTIVES

1. To encourage verbalization of descriptions of the deceased from the homicide survivors.

2. Explore the relationship between deceased and survivor and other family members.

GROUP PROCESS

1. Ask clients to share personal descriptions of the deceased from homework assignment. Expect some to be in great detail, others more general, non-specific traits, e.g., "She was a good mother."

2. Elicit the feelings experienced when writing about the loved one.

3. Acknowledge strengths revealed in the deceased, characteristics now missing in the family system, and validate the void in the family system.

4. Question if other members are attempting to fill the void relating to tasks, functional positions or role of the deceased. "How is that for you?" "Are you expected to fill those roles?" "What does that do to the family?" "To you . . .?"

5. Provide Handout: "Survivors of Homicide Victims," Network Information Bulletin, NOVA, Vol. 2, No. 3, October 1985.

HOMEWORK ASSIGNMENT

1. Write to the deceased telling him of unspoken words, "unfinished business," feelings, thoughts, behaviors that were never expressed, guilt, anger and emotions experienced since the death.

ASSIGNMENT FOR THERAPISTS

1. Read and outline: Lifton (1977) Concept of Modes of Symbolic Immortality.

RATIONALE

Sharing of descriptions of the murdered loved one will re-awaken deep feelings of longing, hurt, and pain. This can renew grief reactions similar to the shock, numbness and denial experienced at the first news of death. The purpose of writing and verbally sharing the descriptions is to enhance acceptance of the reality of the loss. As the client writes about the deceased and speaks to the group of the murdered loved one, the intrapsychic denial of the loss is penetrated.

Those survivors who may not be able to write or speak more than a few descriptive words may be bound intrapsychically so closely to the deceased that they cannot violate this binding. This could be too revealing of *self* and you may hear, "It's too *personal* to share," "She was too *special* to talk about openly to the group."

BE PATIENT. An intrusion too soon, rushing the client, can result in emotional distancing and a closing up of the raw wound of grief you have just begun to open. Also, it is important to remember these clients have experienced a significant invasion of privacy from law enforcement, the criminal justice system, the media, and others due to the nature of the death. Be patient in helping them work through their grief.

A challenge is considered therapeutic at the 9th through 12th sessions, but at this point will only serve to create emotional distance from the pain. The client may leave the group and not return for further help. As a professional, we are responsible for opening the wound of unresolved grief. If left unresolved, this can lead to possible suicide or psychotic depressive illness.

> Meg, 52, had seen a psychiatrist three times after the murder of her son nine years before. She could not stand to speak of him so openly to this stranger. She withdrew into a quiet world of inactivity. Her daughter begged for help for Meg after she told her of plans to end her miserable life. It was an existence based on use of anti-depressants and tranquilizers supplied by the family physician. In group, she was unable to complete the first assignment before the 8th session, then proceeded in a flooding of emotion and anxiety ridden activity. *DO NOT RUSH!*

Acknowledgment of the strengths of the deceased and the realization of the void in the family system due to the death validates the grief reaction. One has a right to grieve, a right to have the sadness, depression and feelings associated with the loss. These do not have to be hidden in the group. For many, the murder will have occurred two-to-ten years earlier. The comments heard from colleagues, co-workers, and family members revolve around chastisement: "Aren't you over that yet?" The void is still a searing pain, and acknowledgment of this by the therapists and other group members leads to recognition of support and understanding and encourages group cohesiveness with identifiable commonalities.

The deceased was an *IMPORTANT* person in the life of the survivor. Recognize the importance of the prior relationship, and how the family system has realigned to fill the functional role of the deceased. As roles, functional positions, and tasks are met by other family members, ambivalence is revealed in anger at the loved one. Sally could not reveal that her father was the black-sheep prior to this examination. Anger is expressed for things such as, "being in the wrong place at the wrong time," "for friends he selected," "being so stupid not to take precautions." Guilt will be expressed that the survivor is angry with the murdered loved one. Guilt is expressed that the survivor is not appreciative of the functional tasks which are now being performed by others. Resentment is expressed that the family expects the survivor to perform some of the roles. These are indications that the survivor is struggling with accepting the reality of the loss and has not *let go* of the deceased.

The feelings of anger and guilt must be verbally expressed. Writing to the deceased will begin to bring into focus some of the issues around which these emotions center. Anger and guilt will be the predominant emotional issues addressed for the next four-to-five sessions.

Therapists must be prepared to be the target of angry outbursts, recognize the need to remain calm, and help survivors to express and discharge this hostility safely. Anger outbursts may also be directed to other group members. Therapists may temper the remarks but generally they are therapeutic when addressed to one another. Anger has been recognized as a predominant feature of the grief process in homicide survivors. This perhaps leads to more marked changes in the personality of the survivor than any other characteristic of homicidal bereavement.

The assignment to write directly to the deceased of "unfinished business" gives the survivor permission to speak unspeakable words; to express guilt, anger, love, other emotions which one has feared to express. Observe how this assignment is directed to "experiencing the pain," as defined by Worden.

The therapist's review of the concepts of introjection and identification assist in being alert to these intrapsychic processes. Observations such as the client not being able to describe particular characteristics of the deceased, seeing the deceased as *Self,* experiencing *Self* as the murder victim, or feelings and expressions of fear and vulnerability as though one will be murdered next, are indicative of this phenomena.

Homicide survivors live with intrusion of thoughts and questions about the thoughts, feelings and behaviors of the murdered loved one in the moments before the death. Years later, this may be expressed as factual data as though it were experienced personally by the survivor, e.g., "she was so frightened, begged for her life," "cried out for me." Questioned if one really knows this, the answer is, "No, but I feel this" (to be true). The therapist will be encouraged to review concepts of self differentiation and to understand the difficulty of decathexis as this process unfolds.

A review of Lifton's five modes of symbolic immortality will provide the therapist the opportunity to understand the meaning of the loss the survivors have experienced. A father is brutally beaten then shot through the head; the son feels compelled to marry and father a child by the same name. A musician's unfinished manuscript must be published by his daughter even at risk of disfavor by the other family members who are saying, "Just get on with your life." The therapist must understand the necessity the survivor feels in seeking to accomplish these goals.

STUDY QUESTIONS

1. What effect does murder (sudden unexpected violent death) have on survivors in relation to Lifton's modes of immortality? How does this differ from anticipated deaths?

2. Read: Rando, (1988), *Grieving: How To Go on Living When Someone You Love Dies,* "Sudden Versus Anticipated Death," p. 89-106.

Session Four

ANGER AND GUILT

OBJECTIVES

1. Explore the relationship with the deceased.

2. Slowly open the "Pandora's Box" of angry and guilt feelings.

3. Forewarn of feeling more depressed. Encourage attendance at all therapy sessions. Review pledge of confidentiality.

GROUP PROCESS

1. Review effects of group grief therapy. How has the sharing, discussions, revealed confidences, support or lack of support affected each member individually?

2. Explore individual relationships with deceased and changes in the family.

3. Review "unfinished business" issues. How did the members feel when writing to the deceased? How difficult is this? Ease in expressing self to deceased in writing? What topics could not be addressed?

4. Encourage writing, recognize difficulty for some members.

HOMEWORK ASSIGNMENT

1. Continue writing directly to the deceased, put into writing your thoughts, feelings, anger, guilt, ambivalence in relationship. Select three focal issues which you never completed with the deceased. End writing with a "Good-bye; I must let you go."

2. Provide handout: Fulton (1984), "Understanding the Experience of Grief."

ASSIGNMENT FOR THERAPISTS

1. Read: van der Kolk, (1984), *Post-Traumatic Stress Disorder: Psychological and Biological Sequelae.*

2. Review: *DSM III-R Manual,* A.P.A. classification 309.8; Post-Traumatic Stress Disorder, Chronic or Delayed.

RATIONALE

By the fourth session, group members may begin to show a normal resistance to continuing in grief therapy. The review of the murder, revealing personal characteristics of the deceased, making observations of ambivalence in the relationship, and openly discussing these issues lead to depression. The client is experiencing emotional exhaustion in the examination of the relationship. Unless strongly motivated to work through the grief process, the member may feel that the resultant depression does not justify the continuation of treatment.

The clients need to realize this process of intricate examination is part of the erosion of restraints. What has brought them to the group is that other methods they tried have not worked. They are now one-third through a process that offers hope in rebuilding their lives. Members need to be forewarned of the depression without setting up a self- fulfilling prophecy and recognize the emotional energy drain which occurs when working through the process. Therapists may address therapeutic methods to handle specific depressive symptoms of individual members.

Through review of what has occurred individually to each, gaining feedback on the group support or lack of support expected, and encouraging individual assistance to all members, the group will be better able to maintain its cohesiveness. Encourage attendance to support one another. Review the pledge of confidentiality established at the beginning of the sessions. A great deal of very personal information has been revealed which could be a source of embarrassment if clients felt it would be openly discussed with other's families. Forewarn members they may continue to feel this emotional exhaustion and depressive symptomatology until they are able to let go of the deceased. This process *CANNOT* be rushed and the group *WILL BE* supportive.

Review of "unfinished business" and continuation of writing directly to the deceased encourages clients to open up communications of thoughts and feelings never discussed before. By now, members are experiencing the realization that writing is helpful, that their most inner thoughts can be committed to paper with no rebuffs. Decisions made during the lifetime of the loved one can be evaluated and confirmed or denied as *right* or *wrong* for them. Writing enhances their observations about the relationship. This leads further into looking at issues where guilt and anger are predominant characteristics.

> Sharon's 27-year-old brother, a drug runner, was murdered by a rival drug dealer gang. He was 15 when their mother died and Sharon took on the role of mother. She had helped him get into college, get an apartment, and spent her hard-earned money buying him clothes and furnishings. She felt a failure for herself, her mother, and brother when he was murdered. Unresolved grief surfaced over her mother's death, and her sense of failure in obligations as a mother to a teenager were intensified. By the fourth session in group therapy she was able to begin the process of forgiving herself, recognizing she had done her best, and that her brother had made decisions which ultimately cost him his life. She slowly turned from the idealization of her brother to a more realistic appraisal and could thereby

express the accumulated anger at him that had been consuming her for years. The love in a relationship lasts forever but the anger can be resolved.

By narrowing the focus to three issues, the griever is given control and empowerment over decision making, e.g., "Which three things about our relationship need to be addressed?" Questioning what cannot be addressed leads to searching for buried resentments and precipitating unresolved issues. By ending the writing with *good-bye,* we begin the process of *leave-taking.* Writing from this point until the completion of therapy will reinforce this closure. The therapists must be aware that this may be premature for some clients and excuse those from completion of this assignment at this time.

The assignment for the therapists to review Post Traumatic Stress Disorder is intended to alert the therapists to symptomatology observable in homicide survivors. The National Organization for Victim's Assistance (NOVA) was instrumental in securing the classification for inclusion in the A.P.A. Diagnostic Manual. It was intended for mass disasters; victim survivors of all crimes; rape, assault, homicide survivors, veterans of wars, and others.

STUDY QUESTIONS

1.   Compare and contrast similarities and differences identifiable in group members using the PTSD classification.

2.   Write these out for each group member.

3.   What parallel behaviors are observable in those group members who are motivated to write and verbally share in the group as opposed to those who are unable to do so? How effective is the use of audiotaping on cassettes when unable to write?

Session Five

ANGER AND GUILT

OBJECTIVES

1. Discuss selected issues from homework assignment.

2. Elicit expressions and feeling level of anger and guilt.

GROUP PROCESS

1. Ask members to share feelings about issues which they selected.

2. Note which issues were selected in order of priority by individual group members.

3. Address individually. Validate each member's priorities.

4. Discuss how anger and guilt have affected members.

HOMEWORK ASSIGNMENT

1. Write out feelings of anger. Begin with statement,"I am angry at . . .," think of anger at murderer, court system, deceased, family members, neighbors, friends, co- workers, any and every identifiable person, object, or system where your anger is directed. Who are "they?" What did they do or leave undone?

2. Provide handout: Bard, Morton, Sangrey (1986), *The Crime Victim's Book,* "Why Me? The Search for a Reason," p. 53-75.

ASSIGNMENT FOR THERAPISTS

1. Read: Lifton (1979), *The Broken Connection On Death and The Continuity of Life,* "Anger, Rage and Violence," p. 147-162; "Survivor Experience and Traumatic Syndrome," p. 163-178.

2. Review: Hankins (1988), *Prescription For Anger: Coping With Angry Feelings and Angry People.*

RATIONALE

Issues of anger will be expressed at every session and are seen as the active struggle against one's own sense of powerlessness. There is deep psychic pain which precedes the anger. There is the sense of one having survived a tearing out of part of one's self, a deep gaping hole remains, bloody, raw and wounded.

The imagery of anger, rage, and violence provides the survivor a way to even the score with the victim for having left, at the murderer for taking the life, and at the complexity of systems which often do not appear to be supportive or satisfy the need for justice.

Lifton (1979, p. 147) suggests that "Anger has to do with a struggle to assert vitality by attacking the other rather than the self." A continuum of anger is described as feeling states combined with anxiety forming an attack imagery moving from anger to rage to violence. The imagery of anger provides a way to act upon the environment rather than be inactivated by the violation. This helps to give meaning and purpose to one's life.

In this session, with the emphasis on confrontation and exploration of anger, ask questions leading to specific issues. Who are you angry at? What did they do? How did you react? What do you wish you had said or done? What can you do now to make a difference? How can you make a difference now with your present knowledge? What actions can be taken?

Through repetitive exploration and examination the survivor begins to reorder the issues recognizing there were things that could have been done differently and others over which one had no control. As the griever makes decisions based on this review there is an **integration** of this experience into one's psyche.

The process of decision making may entail an acceptance of knowing one has done one's best or forgiving self for things left undone or unsaid. Making decisions on actions to take for the present and future gives meaning and purpose to one's life. There may be a renewed determination to find the murderer in an unsolved case, efforts directed to prevent an early parole, attendance and active participation in legislative bodies directed to improving the criminal justice system, or reaching out to other survivors to provide support. These tasks and actions are ones that help provide meaning, a sense of control, and a reason for *being*.

It is strongly suggested that new activity not be started during the process of the grief therapy treatment program. Since the therapy requires a great deal of emotional and physical energy, the griever needs to conserve his efforts directed to therapy. If one starts a new project during therapy, he may become overloaded, thus feel like a failure if the new activity demands even more time and energy than the griever could devote to it. Many survivors begin to formulate future plans between the fifth-to-twelfth session. Encourage them to wait to begin the activity until therapy has been completed. Our purpose is to **empower** the survivor, and there will be a greater chance to reach that goal if progression is carefully graduated.

Therapists are assigned to study literature on the paradigm of anger, rage and violence in order to gain a greater understanding of the process as the clients work to achieve the goal of integration.

STUDY QUESTIONS

1. How does the expression of anger have a therapeutic effect?

2. How do you teach clients to express anger and rage without use of violence? What kinds of expressions of anger must be avoided?

3. Lifton outlines a three-stage process for a survivor of a traumatic situation in "emancipation from the bondage of his own inner deadness." Address each stage in order. How has the work with homicide survivors followed that process? If not, what process do you see occurring in the group?

4. In what way do the concepts that Hankins describes apply to the psychological trauma experienced by homicide survivors? At what point do you believe Hankins concepts would be most useful?

Session Six

FAMILY DYNAMICS

OBJECTIVES

1. Explore the focus of anger described from homework assignment.

2. Examine family relationships; the binding together or tearing apart of the family system as it dealt with the murder of one of its members.

3. Explore how the system selected *the caretaker, scapegoat, responsible one, sick member,* and other functional family roles.

GROUP PROCESS

1. Ask members to share individual reactions from the homework assignment. Note who the anger is directed at within the system.

2. Provide individual genograms to each group member prepared from the initial screening intake session.

3. Ask for a volunteer to share a genogram for review before the group. Draw on the blackboard and ask relationship-related questions.

HOMEWORK ASSIGNMENT

1. Each member is assigned to make an attempt to open communications with one other family member with whom they have had difficulty relating about the murder. This may be accomplished by telephone, in writing, or a personal visit. Encourage the survivor to be an active listener; listen to what is being said, how the other feels, thinks, and has reacted. Encourage the survivor to try not to compare one's own reaction, saving that for further communication.

2. Provide handout: Bard, Morton, Sangrey (1986), *The Crime Victim's* Book, "The Mark: Feelings of Guilt and Shame," p. 76-102.

3. Fill out the evaluation to be handed in at the next session. (see p. 85).

ASSIGNMENT FOR THERAPIST

1. Evaluate course content, the group process, and your progress as a grief therapist. (see p. 86-88).

RATIONALE

The issues of anger and guilt-associated thoughts are discussed from the homework assignment. The confrontation and reordering continues until each issue loses some of its intensity and control. A renewal of self begins to emerge as survivors take action to address the issues. One member relates opening communications with a family member, another checking out police reports that were never seen, another addressing the co-workers who demonstrated they were non- supportive by their actions at the time of the murder. Recognize and validate the actions as opposed to the inactivity and frustrations the member felt previously.

> Alice's 21-year-old daughter was killed instantly in her kitchen by a gunshot wound through the head. The assailant, her boyfriend, then turned the gun on himself. He died in the hospital four days later. His death certificate reported pneumonia as the cause of his death! Alice was furious at this discrepancy. Alice was able to go to authorities, report the facts, and file an official complaint. This action began to change life for Alice who recognized her own ability to influence others. Later, she acknowledged that this might not have been important. But at that time, anger consumed her, and until she filed a complaint, she felt overwhelmed and powerless. This was the beginning of empowerment for Alice.

You may have a member who does not do the homework assignments or reports "its-all-done" when evidence of completing the assignments is lacking. Recognize this as emotional distancing, the withdrawal from pain and resistance. Few people are in grief therapy who have resolved the loss. If available, offer this member individual therapy to explore the resistance and help the client to deal with the pain of grief work. This member denies the pain, continues to idealize the deceased, and cuts off feelings associated with grief. Worden (1982) states that when only pleasant thoughts of the deceased can be acknowledged, this short-circuits the second task of grief work, which is to experience the pain of grief.

The genogram is a useful tool to define the physical and emotional boundaries, characteristics of the membership, toxic issues, emotional cutoffs, and reveals whether the family system is open or closed. Members will identify how they function and fill necessary roles within their individual families. The death will make it evident whether the family deals with issues by being cohesive or explosive. Historically, the majority of homicide survivor families seen in therapy have been *explosive*. A family may have been cohesive prior to the murder but the psychological trauma has resulted in an explosive reactive system. Cohesive families appear to be better able to support their membership and have better coping mechanisms. Explosive families shatter the members into anger pitted at one another. They are unable to assist one another in their grief and have little emotional energy to work on personal relationships.

Group members begin to recognize and understand the part each plays to prevent cohesiveness in their families. They also learn what actions they have taken to protect their own position and sense of self. Those who are motivated to change, will seek further ways to open up communications in their family and change their own position.

At this point in therapy, there may be energy released to address some of the relationship issues. If not, *DO NOT RUSH.* The assignment to write, telephone, or contact a family member lends itself to opening communications. Members are encouraged to become observant and provide a listening ear rather than seek a comparison of "how bad it has been for me." This places the griever in a supportive role.

Each person's grief is unique. Each has been dealing with one's own level of sorrow, guilt, anger, anguish, and pain. Since grief consumes enormous psychological and physical energy, it may be quite impossible to be supportive of others or make changes in the family. The therapist must assess the client's progress individually and not request relationship assignments if the client is not yet ready. More problems can develop in grief therapy from proceeding too quickly than conducting the process slowly.

Sessions seven through twelve are outlined in the following chapter. By the end of the sixth session, therapists will observe various positive changes in the group membership.

Attendance is no longer an issue, as survivors have now established a sense of how helpful this work has been. There is some anxiety concerning what else will be addressed in the upcoming sessions. Some members have experienced a release from the deep painful grip of grief. Others have not yet resolved painful issues, however, by witnessing the dramatic changes in others, feel hopeful as they begin the final sessions of therapy.

A supportive network has formed. By this time, a peer group leader will have emerged who may establish a telephone list of group membership. This is not accomplished earlier or encouraged unless personally requested. Each survivor must work on one's own grief and deal with personal unresolved issues. The members should not be expected to take on the burdens of others until ready. Helping others can be a distancing mechanism to avoid facing one's own painful reality. If one finds himself unable to help others after a concerted effort, the ensuing frustration may lead into a greater sense of despair. The group leader will have to temper planned activity outside the group by encouraging each person to move at one's own pace.

Mid-group evaluations are required at the completion of this session. The evaluation titled "Group Members" is to be completed by the survivors in the group treatment program. Therapists are required to complete evaluations on the course of study, the group process, a self evaluation in the role as group co-leaders, and on the instructor. The evaluations are useless unless the group leader reads them carefully. Discuss pertinent issues with the group members and co-leaders and provide the flexibility to change wherever it may be required. Use the evaluations to direct planned changes in the format, materials, and in conduction of the group process.

MID-GROUP EVALUATION

GROUP MEMBERS

You have now completed six sessions in group grief therapy for survivors of homicide. Please complete this evaluation in order for the therapists to be better able to meet your individual concerns. Review your objectives from Session I.

1.   I have attended _____ sessions.

2.   The group has met my personal objectives. (circle).

   Not At All   *Somewhat*   *As Expected*   *More Than Expected*

3.   The most helpful part of the group has been:

4.   The part I find least helpful and do not like to do:

5.   What I am afraid to do is:

6.   What I wish we could do:

7.   I find the homework assignments: (circle *and* comment).

   Boring; Difficult; Too personal to share; Helpful; Gives me insight into my relationship with deceased; Too painful to complete; Other: (comment).

8.   During the last six weeks I have been able to take action in the area of: (list one action taken. If none, please state).

9.   I have found the therapists to be:

10.   I have found the other group members to be:

11.   Please make any other comments you think will be helpful for the progress and development of the group.

Name (optional)   _____ Date   _____

MID-GROUP EVALUATION

THERAPISTS: You are requested to make comment on the Course Content; the Group Process; Self-Evaluation, and Instructor. Circle the letter which best represents your reaction:

A-Completely;   *B-Satisfactorily;*   *C-Partially*   *D-Not At All*

COURSE CONTENT

1.   The course to train psychotherapists in Group Grief Therapy for Homicide Survivors has been: (include reading assignments, writing assignments, clinical observations).

    a) Too easy . . . . : . . . . A   B   C   D
    b) Basic . . . . A   B   C   D
    c) Material is familiar . . . . A   B   C   D
    d) Inappropriate material . . . . A   B   C   D
    e) Not enough material . . . . A   B   C   D
    f) Difficult . . . . A   B   C   D
    g) Advanced . . . . A   B   C   D
    h) Interesting . . . . A   B   C   D
    i) Appropriate for issues . . . . A   B   C   D
    k) Too much material . . . . A   B   C   D
    l) Other; comment . . . . A   B   C   D

2.   The course has met my objectives in the following:

3.   The course has not met my objectives in:

4.   The assignments which I have found most useful:

5.   The assignments which I have found to be least useful:

6.   My suggestions for improving the quality, quantity, and content of the course are: (please write in detail on back page).

Name   _____ Date   _____

MID-GROUP EVALUATION

GROUP CLINICAL WORK

1.   The environment for the group setting is:

2.   The length of sessions (2 hours) is: (circle and comment).

   Not Enough Time   *Correct Amount Of Time*   *Too Long*

3.   The group process has been:

4.   Are there recurring issues presented during the sessions which have not been anticipated or outlined in the treatment program?

5.   Progress I would like to see occur in the next six sessions:

6.   How can you, as a Group Co-Leader direct and conduct the group to achieve these goals?

SELF-EVALUATION

1.   Please comment on your progress as a Grief Therapist for homicide survivors:

2.   Have you previously treated a client who had experienced a death in the family (from any causes)? Diagnosis:

3.   Has this experience and study been beneficial in your associated work as a therapist? If so, state how. If not, please comment.

4.   Are there mental health issues that survivors have related which were unfamiliar to you prior to this experience? If so, describe:

5.   In designing a course of study to train therapists as leaders of a Homicide Survivors Therapy Group, how would you meet the goals of the therapists?

6.   In what way could the Therapist/Group Leader be more helpful in an effort to help you meet your professional goals?

7.   Other Comments:

Name _____ Date _____

MID-GROUP EVALUATION

EVALUATION OF INSTRUCTOR

1. The instructor's knowledge of the material is:

   Limited   1   2   3   4   5   Excellent

2. The clinical skills of the instructor are:

   Lacking   1   2   3   4   5   Effective

3. The instructor provides:

   Not enough   1   2   3   4   5   More than adequate
   examples   examples

4. The instructor:

   Answers questions   1   2   3   4   5   Answers
   insufficiently   sufficiently

5. The instructor's methods have been:

   Overly simplified   1   2   3   4   5   Challenging

6. Overall this has been a:

   Negative experience   1   2   3   4   5   Very Positive
   Experience

7. Comment on Instructor:

Your candid and open evaluations on the Course in Grief Therapy, Group Process, Self-Evaluation, and Instructor will provide the opportunity to achieve both personal and professional goals. All comments and evaluative scoring will be considered by the Group Leader to promote further progress of the group.

Name (optional) _____ Date _____

*"The world breaks everyone,
then some become strong at the broken places."*
Ernest Hemingway

CHAPTER SIX

Group Grief Therapy Treatment Program Sessions 7-12

This chapter outlines the last six sessions of Group Grief Therapy for homicide survivors. The results of the GEI testing, lessons the author has learned from the groups, and final evaluations are included as part of the last session.

During these sessions some members may resist completion of assignments. There has been such a marked improvement through the last several weeks, clients begin to feel they do not want to do anything to change the gained accomplishments. A feeling of security has developed, the survivor has been acknowledged, encouraged, supported, guided and offered understanding by group members and the therapists. The survivor may have been able to work through the first two tasks of grief work in accepting the reality of the loss and experiencing the pain of grief as described by Worden (1982). Yet the final tasks are undone. In order for the survivor to complete the process of grief work and not abandon the effort, encourage full participation.

Bereavement groups for survivors from other types of death are usually scheduled for six sessions. These are primarily for normalization of grief symptoms and are conducted with an educational focus. These are excellent in meeting the defined goals of that format. The goals for a therapeutic resolution from a complicated bereavement such as experienced in homicide are, however, different. In the experience of HSGP, anything less than twelve sessions of group grief therapy for survivors of homicide has proven insufficient.

The tasks of adjusting to a new environment without the deceased and reinvestment of emotional energy, which are the focal points of these sessions take time, effort, and energy. There may be relationships to repair from damage during angry outbursts, communications to open with other family members, forgiveness of blaming behaviors, a resolution of guilt, a realignment with religious beliefs, the regaining of a sense of control, and becoming empowered in one's life.

These sessions are directed to assisting survivors to reach those goals. As the first six sessions are directed to cleansing the open wound of grief, the latter six are directed to the healing process.

Any changes necessary due to the mid-group evaluations should be incorporated in planning, directing, and conducting these final sessions.

Session Seven

OPENING THE SYSTEM

OBJECTIVES

1. Open communications within the families of the group members.

2. Encourage the realignment of the family system to include all the family members.

GROUP PROCESS

1. With the permission of one member, use a member's family genogram as a model to discuss triangles, money, sex, children, in-laws, religion, or other relationship issues which are pertinent to this group membership. Include discussion of issues such as filling the functional role of the deceased, dependency level of survivor, and ambivalent relationships.

2. Explore the positions of the individual members in their nuclear family. How has this changed since the murder? Was the member emotionally cutoff from the system? How did this occur? Does the member accept or reject this position? Does the member want this to change? Identify those with whom a new alliance could be formed within the family.

3. Discuss how to begin to open a closed family system.

HOMEWORK ASSIGNMENT

1. Contact one family member; continue to explore how the death has affected that person.

2. Identify what issues you react to in a negative manner. Write out one thing you might do to reduce your personal automatic reactivity to the issues.

3. Write out: "What I miss most about . . . (the deceased)." "What I do not miss about . . . (the deceased)."

4. Provide booklet: Osmont, McFarlane (1986) "What Can I Say"?

ASSIGNMENT FOR THERAPISTS

1. Read: Ramsay and Noorbergen (1981), *Living With Loss: A Dramatic New Breakthrough in Grief Therapy.*

RATIONALE

Murray Bowen (1976) defined the concept of "open" and "closed" relationship systems as an effective method in describing death as a family phenomenon.

An open system is one in which members are free to communicate a high percentage of inner thoughts, beliefs, feelings, and fantasies to one another. The closed communication system is governed by an automatic emotional reflex to protect self from the anxiety in the other person. People may say they do not want to upset the other person so avoid the controversial subjects, but this avoidance is to gain self protection from the other's anxiety. When people can follow intellectual knowledge instead of allowing the automatic protective reflex and gain control over their own reactiveness to anxiety in the other, they will be able to talk about taboo subjects. Bowen (1976) states that this provides the opportunity for the relationship to move toward a more healthy openness.

Historically, in working with families after a homicide death, there appears to be a greater number of toxic issues and taboo subject areas than seen in families with other death-related circumstances. Some of the issues are similar: who arranges and attends the funeral, availability and use of support system, mental health of survivors, previous experience with crisis related events, and who died, the *family communicator? the scapegoat? caretaker? good child? trouble-maker? maverick? sick* one? the *family leader? decision-maker?* or one in a less important position within the family?

The family equilibrium will adjust to fill the role and functional position of the deceased. The greater the number of members who take an active part in fulfilling the role and positions, the more cohesive the family. The family becomes more explosive when the roles and functions are assigned, expected, or taken on by only one member. More guilt, blame, anger, resentment, jealousy, and criticisms are expressed in explosive families. An excellent example of this phenomenon was illustrated in session two when Sally took on the roles and functions of her deceased father which resulted in an explosive family system.

The family that has experienced a homicide simply has more issues with which they have to deal, which may become toxic and controversial taboo subjects. Toxic issues revolve around the circumstances of the murder, the apprehension, detention and sentencing of the murderer, and efforts to insure that the sentence is served. Issues that may divide the family are: Who identified the body? How was the identification made? Who was notified following identification? Why were they told before another member? How were they told? Were there other members *protected* until, during, and after the funeral? What members were present during delays for the autopsy report and release of the body from the coroner? Were they critical or supportive of one another? Who came? Who was supportive at the funeral?

Other issues which may be presented are: Who was required to give a deposition? Who came to all the hearings, pre-trial and other proceedings from the beginning? Who was called about the delays? Does one member attend the trial and communicate to the others and, if so, how much information is given? To whom? Families will present many other issues but a key to the closed system is acknowledgment of the family's secrets.

Families who choose to *protect* members by secret-keeping become afraid to talk about any detail of the murder. They are frightened by the anxiety in the other person. That is, what the other person may say, think, or do, if the person knew the details. This leaves a survivor alone and abandoned with only his personal thoughts, feelings, and sense of confusion. The more energy invested into keeping secrets, the less available to work on existing family relationships. Keeping secrets can consume the emotional energy of a family system, energy that could be directed to maintaining open, honest relationships. Those who are privy to *the secret* begin to doubt if *we* are keeping this from *her,* what are *they* keeping from me? It can lead to paranoia, self-doubt, self-blame, loss of control, feelings of vulnerability, fear, and increased emotional distance. Secrets are damaging to the psyche of the individual, and to the mental health of the family as it relates to the social community.

> The mother of five children experienced symptoms of severe confusion and disorientation 18 months after the murder of her 24-year-old son. The mother was aware of emotional withdrawal of every family member since the murder of her youngest child. The family had chosen to not tell Mother her son was murdered in a gay bar. She had no access to, or knowledge of how to get police or coroner's reports. The other children and father thought Mother would die of shame to find out that her son was gay. The family "protected " her from the secret. No one in the family would talk to her about her murdered son. The eldest son and one daughter became emotionally cutoff from the family.
>
> The mother became more anxious, confused, depressed, and, at intake into the group, was in severe despair. She had suicidal ideation expressed as "the only way out." She was experiencing nightmares, unable to function at work, sleep, or eat adequately. A family physician had continued to prescribe sleep medication for the entire 18 months!
>
> Within four sessions in the HSGP Group Grief Therapy Treatment Program she became determined to find out the details of her son's murder. She arranged to visit the investigating detective and dealt with the information openly with all the family members. She reopened what had become a closed family system. The stigmatized death by murder in a gay bar no longer divided the family but served to unite them after Mother took decisive action.
>
> The nightmares ceased, she began sleeping without medication, eating normally, her appearance and affect were markedly improved.

SECRET KEEPING IS DAMAGING TO EMOTIONALLY HEALTHY FUNCTIONING! Those who choose to protect others from truths and realities do a great disservice. It becomes impossible to resolve the relationship with the deceased and leads to distancing from surviving family members. Secrets can destroy marriages, family relations, social and community interrelations. Do not be afraid to question "Who are you to determine what she has the right to know?" We must not set ourselves up as more able to deal with realities than others. Secrets deny everyone involved the right and opportunity to reach out for support.

The assignment for therapists is directed to study information about the use of Guided Confrontation Therapy as practiced by Ramsay and Noorbergen. These practitioners use techniques of grief therapy in a short period of time. One case relates work done in a six-day period, taking the person to the edge of an emotional psychotic break. They report excellent results with their methods of confrontation. In the HSGP Group Grief Therapy Treatment Program, many of the same techniques are recommended, but used over a much longer time period. The internalized process of decathexis requires a much longer duration of time. The internalized struggle to separate one's self from the deceased is not accomplished easily. It takes time to resolve all the complexities and complications of a relationship, particularly with a deceased loved one who has been murdered.

STUDY QUESTIONS

1. How do the methods used in Guided Confrontation Therapy compare to Grief Therapy presently being used with this group? What techniques are similar? Note differences.

Session Eight

AMBIVALENCE AND REBUILDING RELATIONSHIPS

OBJECTIVES

1.   Acknowledge ambivalence in relationship with the deceased.

2.   Support member as discovery and self-awareness becomes acknowledged and integrated pertaining to: How member was selected for new role by the system?

3.   Explore with member, the desire to function in new role. What actions would be necessary to change this position in the family?

GROUP PROCESS

1.   Review issues which became apparent when members wrote out assignment from previous week. "What I miss most about . . ." and, "What I don't miss about . . . (the deceased)." Ask, "How did it feel to write out the assignment?"

2.   Ask questions to clarify functioning of new role. Is it necessary in this family to have a *problem member?* As *caretaker* do you feel responsible to communicate to all extended family or just a dyad/triad of members? How do you see the new family rules of communication? What changes are apparent? Have you been emotionally cutoff from the system? What changes would you have to make to reestablish a connection with the system?

3.   Ask questions regarding functional roles within the family. How do you function in this position in the family? Are you resentful of other family members' expectations of you? Do you feel overloaded, ill-at- ease, over-responsible for others? Could you allow them to make their own decisions? What would that do to the family system?

4.   Announce and prepare membership for the next session on funerals, be supportive but encourage full participation.

5.   Announce Memorial Service session which will be held in Session 10. This allows time for anticipation, preparation for, and planning of a service which the survivors feel to be appropriate. Due to the shock sequela, homicide survivors were denied this type of control and planning in their earlier experience.

HOMEWORK ASSIGNMENT

1. Write out what happened at the funeral, who was there, who did not attend, who was most helpful, least helpful, what was said or done that helped the most, hurt the most?

2. Write out a fantasy of what could have been done differently at the funeral.

3. Provide handout: "The Function of Funerals."

ASSIGNMENT FOR THERAPISTS

1. Read: Rando (1984), *Grief, Dying, and Death,* "Funerals and Funerary Rituals," p. 173-197.

2. Read: Stephenson (1985), *Death, Grief, and Mourning,* "Ceremonies of Death: The Funeral," p. 198-234.

RATIONALE

Relationships are explored, defined and clarified in ambivalent terms as the group discusses the assignment of "What I miss most about . . . and what I don't miss." Members are frequently shocked to realize their list of "What I don't miss" is longer, in more detail, and required more time to write.

IT IS VERY IMPORTANT THAT THIS ASSIGNMENT NOT BE DONE OR REFERRED TO EARLY IN GRIEF THERAPY! The survivor must be comfortable with having verbalized the *idealized* deceased. The writing process will be threatening and produce feelings of guilt and shame if the member has yet to describe who died, explore their relationship, how the deceased fit into the family, how the family has realigned, and the survivor's own role and functional position. This is similar to beginning a narrow focus, then widening the lens to include all the family, then returning to re-explore the one-on-one relationship with the murder victim. This will assist in the transformation of the mental imagery of the physical presence of the deceased into reality-oriented memories that one can live with.

The other group members and therapists have heard about the capabilities, accomplishments, and worthwhile future hopes and dreams of the *good* person who died. The mental imagery of the person is accepted but is insufficient and lacks clarity without the total picture of the deceased as being human. Everyone has both positive and negative qualities. For the survivor to be released from the ties that bind the survivor to the dead, mental imagery of the real person must be revived and reviewed in a realistic frame of reference. This cognitive restructuring is done in an atmosphere of acceptance within the group.

Verbalization of the ambivalent feelings may result in venting angry emotions about personality, actions, behaviors, thinking, and feelings about the deceased. The survivor recognizes both the positive and negative qualities, and the reality that the deceased was a normal person. It is easier to live with memories of a normal human being.

This verbalization leads to forgiveness of self for things the survivor did or did not do in the relationship. Irrational guilt feelings are relieved as group members respond to one another about difficulties each experienced in their relationships.

> A 37-year-old woman had defended every action of her 38-year-old lover who was the father of her children and who had been murdered in an alcoholic rage by a neighbor. In this session she felt it safe to share that she had chosen to leave him only a few weeks prior to the murder because of the negative influence he had on the children due to his alcoholism. She was supported by the group in her decision. She began the road to recovery when she recognized she was not ostracized for having lived with, loved, and left an alcoholic. Her grief was acknowledged and accepted as normal.

The survivor may have resolved many personal issues with the deceased at this point in therapy. Things said or done in earlier experiences have been revived, reviewed, and examined in a different frame of reference. The examination of what has occurred in other family relationships which may sound repetitive to the reader must continue. To the therapist these actions and subject matter are not repetitive until the griever responds by making concrete decisions, once again taking control of one's life.

In order to adjust to an environment where the deceased is missing, as suggested by Worden (1982), the survivor must acknowledge the changes in the system and his part in them. After the last two sessions, group members become amazed as they begin to identify how the system chose them for their new functional role. Continue to ask questions to clarify the requirements of the role. What actions, behaviors and messages does the survivor use to communicate acceptance or rejection of the role? Does the survivor *choose* to continue to function in the role?

> Greg, 43, a well-educated computer analyst was unemployed when he was admitted to the HSGP Group Grief Therapy Treatment Program. Eleven years earlier his father was brutally beaten and murdered. Greg's stepmother had hired "hit men" to kill his father. Greg, the eldest of four children, was in the first year of his marriage, attending a prestigious graduate school in a distant state at the time of the murder.
>
> Afterwards, he was asked by his siblings to come home to help with the family business. Greg had spent his life seeking his father's approval and "knew" that in returning home, it would be what his father would have wanted. His father had been the family decision maker, the powerful head of a large family clan, well known and respected as a successful businessman in the community. As the eldest son, Greg accepted the leadership role. He felt obligated to live in an area which he had not chosen, doing work which was neither in his area of interest nor expertise.

His marriage failed. The family business folded within two years. He worked sporadically for several companies but spent his time and energy focused in anger at the court system which continued considering parole for the murderess. He felt it was his obligation to represent the family. Greg spent his spare time seeking employment which never materialized, counseling his brothers and sister, and maintaining the role of family leader and caretaker.

He chose to give up the role of surrogate father to his siblings midway through the therapy sessions. Less than a week after the last session, Greg telephoned with news of obtaining a full-time position in middle management with a computer firm. He had become aware of his own acceptance of a role he never chose. The group provided the support and encouragement to become his own man again. In his words, "I realized (that) it was my father who was murdered, not me!"

In this case, as in many homicide cases, there is evidence of strong identification with the victim. A major goal of grief therapy is to assist survivors in individuation of self from the deceased.

The assignment for group members and therapists in training leads into a review of funerals for the following session.

STUDY QUESTIONS

1. What is the purpose of funerals in our society?

2. Address the difficulties survivors of homicide experience during funerals. Consider identification of the deceased, delays due to a coroner's examination, emotional state, crisis intervention theory, intrusion by other systems, anxious systems, and value of funerals and rituals.

Session Nine

REVIEW OF FUNERAL

OBJECTIVES

1.   To review the funeral in order to place it into a constructive perspective.

2.   To reduce confusion of thought. Dozens of separate issues which often are labeled the "funeral" may need to be examined.

3.   To recognize that some of the things that were done or said, or not done or said, were the very best others were capable of at that time, place, and in those circumstances.

4.   To review what "I wish I had done"; verbal expression and sharing with group provides an outlet to reduce anxiety, unfulfilled expectations of self, and allows others to know of good intentions.

5.   To share anger that members feel could not be appropriately expressed at time and place of the funeral.

GROUP PROCESS

1.   Discuss difficulty of reliving the funeral.

2.   Discuss emotions generated when writing this assignment.

3.   Examine resistance from some members for whom the funeral is a source of buried resentment, rage, or constricted due to the shock and numbness at the time. Explain that this review could help cleanse the wound of emotional pain and provide a way to put those tragic memories to rest.

4.   Review the thought process of, "What I wish I had done differently."

5.   Explore what actions you can take now; e.g., offer a Mass, write a family member, accept responsibility for your actions and feelings at the time, write a friend, or plan a memorial in keeping with unfulfilled expectations and desires.

HOMEWORK ASSIGNMENT

1.   Plan a memorial service for the deceased.

2.   Bring in a picture of the deceased to share in group memorial service.

ASSIGNMENT FOR THERAPISTS

1. Review: Morgan (1984), A *Manual of Death Education and Simple Burial,* "Sample Death Ceremonies," p.122-142.

2. Read: Volkan (1981), *Linking Objects and Linking Phenomena,* "Re-Grief Therapy," p. 201-233.

RATIONALE

The funeral review is dreaded by group members when originally assigned. Members will profess they "cannot go through that," "do not remember," "will miss that session," and other messages of resistance. In the experience of HSGP, counting all the group treatment programs, only one member did not come to the funeral session. Encourage the members to attend, participate, and share if possible. If unable to share, just listening to others will revive buried memories this event elicits. Every member who completes the assignment and has been able to verbalize the events evaluates this session as one of the most rewarding of the treatment program. It cannot be held earlier for fear of possible repression of the painful memories.

One member remarked, "I had not known how angry I was with my family before this." She achieved understanding of her family's actions. Another said, "We often speak of births, first holy communion, bar mitzvah, graduation exercises, weddings, but we never talk about burying Mother after she was murdered!"

Survivors express anger experienced due to the delay of the funeral, memories of the media blitz, police actions, medical examiners report, and other issues which are cognitively tied into the actual funeral service itself. The work of the therapist is to filter the confused mass of memories and guide the griever to transform the confusion into ordered thought processes.

The funeral review will include, but not be limited to: discovery of the deceased; notification of the family; the way the deceased was removed from the murder site; whether the survivor was allowed within the confines of the restricted murder scene; how police detectives responded to survivors; response of the media to the family; cleaning up the murder scene; being able to see the deceased before burial or cremation; attendance of family members and others before, during, and after the funeral service; response of the church or religious leaders; requests for or denial of special prayers or readings; what was actually said or done by others in sending messages of support, associated shame and stigma; burial or cremation of the loved one.

It is obvious that much more could be written on each one of the above issues. Only those which are generally difficult to locate in other references will be addressed. It will be helpful for the therapist to read Pine (1976), *Acute Grief and the Funeral.*

One of the most difficult memories for many survivors is the cleaning up process after the *professionals* leave the scene. The body has been removed, the house may be filled with black dusting for fingerprints, pools of dried blood, cut off carpet and dried tissue spattered on cabinets, furniture, and walls. The house, or a particular area, may be in disarray due to a struggle, pilfered, and broken treasures scattered about. *REMEMBER, THIS IS THE LIFE BLOOD OF SOMEONE'S LOVED ONE!* It is not some murder mystery solved in a 30-minute television time slot with neat clean gestures.

Associated implications are crucial to the resolution of grief. Unfortunately, cleaning crews do not come from the police departments. Many professional cleaning services are ill equipped to clean up after a suicide or homicide, or, the cleaning service will offer to schedule the service, as though it is an activity that can be placed on a calendar for one day the following week, or the service will send their most inexperienced, newly hired workers. (On one occasion the writer spent the greater part of time and effort in care of a 17-year-old cleaning crewman who got ill at the sight of blood.)

The mother of a murdered daughter said, "I do not know what all I did that week. I remember spending hours scrubbing blood off of the kitchen floor and cabinets. When it was clean I would scrub it again. I knew I must be calm for the other children. Later I wondered, did anyone know how terrible I felt? I had been too good and forced back the tears."

Another issue in which there is a lack of sufficient research and inconclusive knowledge is the importance of viewing the body of the deceased. Yet, in over 280 homicide cases in the author's experience, the survivors, who were not allowed to view the body, question, "Was it really my (loved one)?" The police, family members who identified the body, funeral directors, and others, often decide *to protect* the closest of kin by insisting they not visually see the deceased. Years later, this issue keeps surfacing as one of the most traumatic of the death. We must visually see death to integrate the reality into our psyche.

On one occasion, the funeral director creatively turned the body in the casket so only the lower trunk and legs could be viewed. Lower lighting, use of veils, and other creative methods can be employed. If the survivor can only see one finger of the hand, or any part of the body, it will help to answer this terrible intrusive, repetitive, incessant question. No matter how terrible the decomposure, within reason, it cannot compare to the mental imagery of horror possibly visualized by the survivor who has been denied a viewing. For most people, the imagination is worse than reality.

Those who have been denied a viewing harbor greater anger at the persons responsible for that decision. They also express guilt that they were unable to make that decision for themselves. It is another example of an issue where the survivor experiences loss of control, feeling powerless in that others took the control from them. *IN YOUR TEACHING, INSIST ON PERSONAL VIEWING OF THE DECEASED!*

> A mother said, "I saw my naked child at birth, how dare they prevent me from seeing his face, just to touch him one more time, I cannot believe I couldn't see him dead, that was my right as his mother!" Later her comments turned to guilt that she could not make the decision without the influence of others. "I am ashamed of me that I didn't make the decision to see him regardless of what others said."

Despite experiencing the shock and numbness of the first reaction to the murder, the difficulty in making decisions, the experience of angry outbursts, and stunned feelings, many survivors report a photographic memory of details of the event. Many of these memories have been buried and confused in the mass of unresolved issues. As the survivor writes and verbalizes the details, this confusion clears and the funeral takes on a new meaning as a tribute to the loved one.

It is important to review what the survivor wishes could have been done differently regarding the funeral service. Anger and guilt may be expressed that other family members made decisions believed to be inappropriate for the service. Visualizing the funeral in review helps the griever put the issues in perspective. Sharing this information provides an outlet to reduce anxiety, and makes the good intentions of the griever public. After this session, a member said of a prayer which was requested but neglected at the funeral service, "It's alright now that I didn't say it there because sharing it here with the group, I know it's said." The value of acknowledgment is apparent in this statement.

Another young wife reviewed a promise she had made to her husband of five months that neither wanted a Catholic Mass and whoever was left at death would see to it that a simple service with cremation would be held for the other. At the time of funeral planning his family gathered and made the decision that a Mass in the Catholic Church, which was desired by the parents, was the most appropriate service. The wife felt helpless, harbored irrational rage, and felt she had betrayed her husband by being part of and not preventing this form of service. Through the review she was able to release the anxiety provoking guilt, cognitively restructure the event, forgive others responsible for the final decisions, and accept that what had been done was appropriate under the circumstances. Lifton (1979) refers to the necessity of guilt-associated struggles centering around the responsibility to the dead and the experience of one's own inner deadness without which renewal cannot be achieved. The wife's ability to confront and reorder the event in her thinking provided a sense of renewal which led to an open discussion with his family and subsequent development of understanding between them. The families had needed yet denied one another support prior to this. Afterwards, they began to rebuild their relationship with one another.

The next session is provided as the opportunity for survivors to do those things which were desired yet left undone at the funeral service. The assignment for group members should be given two weeks earlier for ample preparation time. The reading assignment for therapists will provide basic knowledge on memorial services. Therapists should be knowledgeable about the value of rituals in order to prepare adequately for the next session.

STUDY QUESTIONS

1. What is the value of a memorial service in honor of a deceased loved one?

2. Describe "Re-Grief Therapy" as practiced by Volkan.

3. What is a linking object? In what way can you as a therapist assist the client in decathexis by use of an identified linking object?

Session Ten

MEMORIAL SERVICE

OBJECTIVES

1.   To offer a personalized memorial tribute to the deceased loved one.

2.   To publicly recognize the positive attributes of the murder victim.

3.   To focus on the present, recognizing that memories of the loved one will not diminish. The history and meaning of the life shared will be integrated into the future of the survivor.

GROUP PROCESS

1.   Allow group members to organize the setting and format by arranging seating, setting up table or display area for photographs of deceased, taking own initiative in conducting the memorial service.

2.   Therapist may plan to take part by lighting a candle for each honored deceased or share in service in a therapeutic, participatory manner.

HOMEWORK ASSIGNMENT

1.   Write out, "What I fear the most now is . . ."

ASSIGNMENT FOR THERAPISTS

1.   Prepare evaluations for group members to be handed out at next session.

2.   Read: Osterweis, M., Solomon, F. and Green, M., eds. *Bereavement Reactions, Consequences and Care,* (1984) "Adult's Reaction to Bereavement" p. 47-68; "Reactions to Particular Types of Bereavement" p. 71-95; "Bereavement Intervention Programs," p. 239-277.

RATIONALE

The memorial service session is designed to provide an opportunity for the griever to publicly acknowledge some of the most cherished memories of the deceased. As the funeral session focused on the past, the memorial session centers on a *here-and-now* reality.

Prayers, poems, verse, writings created by or about the loved one, taped music, and other renditions may be used in the sharing. Encourage the group members to be creative and share whatever is most meaningful to them.

Members may be highly anxious and express resistance to this session. They express concern in fear of "not doing it right" "not being able to say enough," and other comments. *BE FIRM, PATIENT, CARING, BUT INSISTENT ON ATTENDANCE.* If grievers choose not to share, be accepting of the limitation. The session provides an opportunity for members to make decisions in selection of materials and choosing what to say. This establishes a renewed sense of control. Members will often have worried concern and lament over choices yet each will express satisfaction once they have presented their tribute.

Another issue which is addressed in this session concerns the ambivalence which had been brought out in earlier sessions. Negative qualities and anger at the deceased were brought out when grievers wrote out "What I don't miss" about the loved one. The memorial service reaffirms positive loving memories the member feels for one's loved one. This serves to reduce guilt feelings one may experience from having shared negative qualities.

This is one of the most intense, personal sessions of the treatment program in grief therapy. It is during the preparation for this session that the "grief work" will be accomplished. Some of the most creative and beautiful tributes I have ever witnessed were presented in these sessions by homicide survivors. Each tribute is presented with a deep level of personal meaning. A few examples of memorials follow in order to assist therapist in explaining the assignment to survivors.

One mother in preparation, reviewed all the sympathy cards received. In the process of reading the cards she identified the importance of personal written messages by others. She chose one particularly meaningful verse penned by a family friend which had deep meaning for her in honoring her daughter. She had also purchased a favorite plant which would flower during the month of her daughter's death. During the week she had reviewed and packed away the sympathy cards, the autopsy and court reports in a cedar chest. These are to be shared with her five-year-old grandson (who witnessed his mother's murder) when he is older. She remarked, "We try to put things behind us, but for the first time this really made me look ahead . . . It felt good to put things away."

Another member, in honoring her father who had been a jazz musician, played his music all day working on the selections she chose to tape on cassette for the memorial. Prior to this she had been unable to listen to his music. Now, with the purpose of sharing her father's recordings, she was able to once again hear and love the sounds of his trumpet. This was difficult, but she accomplished a long-awaited goal.

A member chose to share a personal story of an early remembrance of her mother who was the murder victim. They had lived in a small town in the northeast and in the early spring all the girls decided to wear white shorts one day. As a young teenager she had told mother at bedtime that she needed a pair of white shorts for the following morning. It was of paramount importance! Mother had said there was just no way to buy any at the late hour and she did not sew. Nevertheless, the next morning the white shorts, sewn less than perfectly by hand, were laid out on her bed. Sharing this story of the kind of loving, caring, and understanding person her mother had been gave the griever tremendous group support in her grief. She brought memories alive of the person her mother had been and, in writing this memory, knew that her mother would always be a treasured part of her life.

A member read the Twenty-Third Psalm which she had requested at her son's funeral. She had resented that the priest had not complied with the request. Sharing it with the group now two years after the funeral fulfilled that need and desire for the surviving mother.

A young adult wrote all the special memories of things she enjoyed most about her dad, beginning each statement with ''The way you . . . .''

One recited a Hebrew prayer, explaining the meaning to his group.

Each person shares treasured photographs which serve to refresh memories. The verbal sharing confirms that memories will never be forgotten and can become a cherished part of life. This also gives sanction to approach the future without fear or guilt that the deceased loved one will be forgotten.

As part of the service, the group leader may light a candle in remembrance of each person for whom the members grieve. It is suggested to practice this ritual and offer a few words of impressions gained about the deceased from the members. It is a privilege to share in the life of the survivor's deceased loved ones and join in honoring the victims during this tribute.

One member said she carried her candle with her throughout the approaching holidays. Then, lit it in each relative's home where she visited. This helped lift the feelings of gloom for everyone because the missing child was recognized and honored.

At the end of this ceremony, photographs of the loved ones are hung on the memorial wall in the HSGP office. The group members have shared their living and their dying, and leave this recognition and acknowledgment for all to share.

This is also a session which survivors evaluate as one of the most rewarding. It is very difficult at the time, but is invaluable in the benefits gained by the group members.

The assignment to write out ''What I fear most now'' is designed to address any other unresolved issues and focus on the future.

Therapists should prepare evaluation forms to be handed out to group members at Session Eleven.

STUDY QUESTIONS

1.   Describe your concepts of an adult's reaction to bereavement. Note the differences for particular types of death.

2.   Based on your knowledge and experience, formulate and address three research questions on Bereavement Intervention Programs. How would this research be of value?

Session Eleven

UNFINISHED BUSINESS

OBJECTIVES

1. Address unresolved issues. These may include but not be limited to: the relationship to the deceased, death by murder, reconfirming religious beliefs or accepting changes in beliefs due to the violation, criminal justice system, other family relationships, new employment directions, and plans for the future.

2. Acknowledge the level of anxiety expressed by group members as they plan to complete therapy the following week.

GROUP PROCESS

1. Request sharing of fears identified from the homework assignment.

2. Support group members in plans for their future.

HOMEWORK ASSIGNMENT

1. Pass out evaluation forms. Encourage group members to complete evaluations as required homework. (see p. 117).

ASSIGNMENT FOR THERAPISTS

1. Complete all assignments and written work not previously turned in to group leader.

2. Read: Rando (1986), *Parental Loss Of A Child,* p. 5-119; 341-413.

RATIONALE

The homework assignment of "What I fear most now" reveals a wide range of issues. This leads the griever into a future oriented focus. For those in situations where the killer is still at large, fear for their safety and of a possible confrontation, should he be found, is expressed. There is a sense of dread of the activities they know they must endure in the legal prosecution, yet they are eager to seek justice. Some fear the first parole hearing of the murderer. When the killer has legally exhausted all appeals and is incarcerated with a life sentence, survivors are better able to focus on their own future. In several HSGP cases, the murderer committed suicide following the murder. These survivors reciprocally show less fear for their future.

Most survivors desire to improve the criminal justice system from which they have suffered multiple secondary victimization. Some who have gained knowledge of the system prepare plans to meet with responsible authorities and complete individual concerns. Others begin to collect records and documentation, simply to pack away, and strive to seek a life void of the reminders of the victimization.

Some members review earlier family death experiences and share how they have been able to complete grief work on these unresolved relationships. Members report that communications have been opened within their own family system. Yet, many still experience resentment that friends and co-workers are unable to understand and share this crucial aspect of their life. Some make plans for public education programs and promote community awareness through personal presentations.

Writing out their fears and verbalizing these within the group helps members to focus on priorities. The renewed sense of control is evident as members review selected options, make choices, and discuss the issues with one another. For those who choose a new direction, the group provides a firm supportive system.

This session reaffirms reorganization of renewed energy and personal plans for the future. The task described by Worden (1982) of adjusting to an environment where the deceased is missing and reinvestment in other relationships becomes apparent. A widow had her first date shortly after the completion of her therapy. For some, the new relationship will encompass investment of emotional energy into making positive changes in our systems of justice so that others who follow will find a less difficult path.

It was at this particular session in the winter of 1986 that the homicide survivors in the pilot program determined that they would do whatever was necessary so that other survivors would have access to the treatment program. The group discussed plans to be trained as volunteers to assist newly-bereaved survivors. One member made arrangements with a cleaning service who agreed to respond appropriately to the needs of surviving families. Plans were made for fund raising so other survivors who are unable to pay for the treatment program could have access to therapy free-of-charge. The group members set the groundwork which later became an incorporated, non-profit organization staffed by volunteers and directed by a professional therapist. It became evident the group members were committed to continue in their support of one another through formation of a mutual peer support group. The preparation to end the group became a new beginning with a renewed focus to help others.

STUDY QUESTIONS

1.   Address difficulties of the parental loss of a child. Compare this to other losses studied.

2.   Complete evaluations. Compare your objectives for course of study and clinical training; personal and professional goals with objectives prior to course.

Session Twelve

EVALUATION AND TERMINATION

OBJECTIVES

1. Evaluate each individual group member's progress and the total group process.

2. Evaluate the clinical work of therapists in training.

3. Complete group process with reinforcement of empowerment for each individual.

4. Terminate group with closure for each member and therapist.

5. Provide Grief Experience Inventory post-test.

6. Complete a self-evaluation as group leader.

GROUP PROCESS

1. Provide at least 30 minutes to administer Grief Experience Inventory post-test instrument.

2. Compare the personal objectives written out at first session to evaluative comments. Did each member meet personal objectives?

3. Discuss evaluative comments written on final evaluation forms.

4. Request each member to identify what actions, comments, and feelings expressed by other members were most helpful. What was done or said that hurt or angered one another but helped to resolve conflicts of grief?

5. Therapists are to address each member with statement of: "What you have taught me."

6. Prepare members to recognize that future time together may not be at level of emotional depth experienced in the group. Allow time for parting and *goodbyes*.

ASSIGNMENT FOR THERAPISTS

1. Review evaluations. Collate materials; examine for patterns, note similarities and differences.

2. Arrange to review filming, audio recordings, and individual therapist evaluations.

3. Prepare for next group, using evaluative summaries as guidelines.

RATIONALE

The Grief Experience Inventory post-test is provided at this final session. After the group leader collates results, schedule individual interviews with each group member to review the comparison between pre-test and post-test results.

As mental health professionals, we are responsible to evaluate the progress and results of our services. Progress is measurable in attainment of clearly defined objectives.

The group members may read or comment on the objectives each one defined for themselves at the start of therapy. Group members most often evaluate the group treatment experience as more than expected. A member relates, "The group took the murder out of the death. . . . I was so hung up on the murder I had not truly grieved for my mother being dead. Everyday I wonder who did it and why, but the pain of grief is gone."

Each member has shared some of the deepest, most personal emotional turmoil of their lives with one another in the group. Revealing oneself to another can result in feelings of vulnerability. The trust which has been placed in one another is reinforced by the weekly sharing and the mutually working through the grief process. Now at termination, each one needs an affirmation of the value of that trust from one another. Thus, asking each to share how others have helped reinforces a strong positive self-image. The survivor is acknowledged in both group roles, as the active giver, and passive receiver of care.

It is also important to provide the opportunity for members to discuss their conflictual issues. The group will be made up of diverse personalities with divergent viewpoints. Some of the seething anger is now tempered with understanding. One member in a group said to another, "I hated you when you said, 'Well what do you want' in remarks about (my husband), later I realized that's what made me go to him and tell him what I needed." Another said, "If you had not told me you hated your husband, I would not have known I was normal." There are many remarks of reinforcement for the help each has provided to one another. The opportunity to model conflict resolution through open communication is consistently reinforced.

The HSGP group members have been most supportive of one another. Each group selects the *"MOST IMPROVED."* A member said, "You keep seeing the change in everyone else, then suddenly realize you've had a really good day and you're not crying anymore. It must be happening to me, too!"

Therapists are requested to share what they have learned with the group membership. A composite of observations which have been gained from the HSGP groups are on the following pages.

Acknowledgment of what the members have taught group leaders provides recognition to the survivors for their willingness to be our teachers. This leads to a renewed sense of empowerment. The group has experienced psychological trauma unlike any other. They have been tested beyond all normal limitations. To observe the power and strength of the human spirit and development of the coping abilities witnessed in survivors is most inspiring. This is a difficult, complex bereavement reaction but can be resolved through group grief therapy. Homicide survivors are willing teachers if we, as practitioners, are willing to listen and learn from them.

LESSONS LEARNED FROM THE GROUPS

Working with groups of homicide survivors has reinforced the belief that one of the major differences in grief reactions is due to a conflict in values and beliefs. Belief in a just-and-fair society and the high value placed on life becomes shattered when the survivor experiences the murder of a loved one. Subsequently, a court system that provides *justice* for the criminal but not for the family of the victim is conflictual. Further, the perception of the minimal value of a victim's life is reflected in a short confinement for the murderer. The mind simply cannot tolerate or absorb the conflict these issues create. Either everything one has been taught to believe is wrong, or the present reality is wrong.

The desire and intent to gain retribution is not only normal but necessary. This needs to be explored and discussed. The survivor may be able to forgive the murderer but still expects punishment for the criminal act. The guilt which results from the desire for retribution creates emotional distancing that in turn leads to damaged interpersonal relationships. This is a subject which requires further study and research.

If the murderer is still free, or the case unsolved, grief can still be resolved. The grief process resolves the loss of the person in one's life. This does not negate the necessity of apprehension and punishment of the criminal.

If the known murderer is free, has never served time, or was freed on court technicalities, the survivor continues to live with a sense of imbalance, loss of control, and constant fear. However, grief therapy still serves to mitigate the lost relationship.

If the murderer served minimal time, (one-year-and-a-day cases), the survivor continues to experience resentment at the injustice. Several HSGP group members have made the decision to bring civil suits in these cases. Grief therapy is still effective, however, in the resolution of the loss relationship.

When the murderer committed suicide or was killed after the act of homicide, anger at the system was lessened. It appears that other systems had less opportunity to create secondary victimization for the survivors. These survivors had a less complicated bereavement reaction considering other factors.

If the murderer is incarcerated with little to no chance of parole or has exhausted all appeals, the survivor is better able to direct all renewed energy to focusing on a new direction in life.

Survivors experience a greater sense of anger, fear, violation, and powerlessness when the murder was brutal. Body mutilation of a loved one appears to result in a stronger identification with the deceased. This experience results in the survivor losing more control of one's personal life and environment.

Those survivors who presented with strong overt religious beliefs had more conflict than those who were less vociferous about their religion. It appears the devoutly religious were conditioned to expect more support and experienced a greater sense of abandonment from their church. They felt betrayed by their belief system which offered little comfort. Platitudes such as "It was God's will," "Those who live by the sword will die by the sword," "Be Better not Bitter," offered by clergy and others were inadequate and resented. There is a need for continued education in grief for the clergy and other care providers.

Once the anger and rage is initially spent, it is not subsequently seen at the level previously experienced. The exhaustion resulting from difficult grief work is apparent, and the mood and affect of the griever is one of relief and release. A member said on the release of anger, ''I felt like I vomited bile!''

As therapists, mental health professionals, death educators, bereavement counselors, victim advocates and others who intend to help homicide survivors, *DO NOT FEAR EXPRESSIONS OF ANGER*. These expressions are appropriate for the psychological trauma experienced.

Expressions of guilt are more difficult for the survivor to resolve than those of anger. It is the confrontation, and subsequent reordering, that makes it possible to relieve oneself of the guilt. The group work lends itself to this process.

The process of grief therapy can resolve delayed, complicated bereavement even if the murder occurred years earlier. As in some of the HSGP cases, the murder may have occurred as many as 12-15 years earlier.

Every survivor of homicide makes the therapist aware of the invaluable need for acknowledgment, education, support, love, caring, and consideration.

EVALUATIONS

Subjective evaluations were gained from personal observations by the group leader and co-leaders. Survivors present an array of physical and emotional symptomatic behaviors at intake. There was evidence of impeded functioning in interpersonal relationships, social and community interactions, and employment relations. Forty-six members out of 50 who have completed the treatment program show a marked change in higher functioning in each of the areas.

Four members continued to experience difficulties that were not resolved by the group grief therapy. Two exhibited borderline personality disorders that were not evident, or missed, in the assessment at screening intake. Both dropped out of the group in their respective fourth session. One survivor later returned for individual grief therapy. The other was referred for psychotherapy at a local mental health agency. Two other clients completed the sessions, but could not complete the assignments. The mother of a child who died by acute alcohol poisoning felt at intake that this was murder due to coercion by others. She was overwhelmed by the stories of other survivors and later felt she could not identify herself as a homicide survivor even though her group had been supportive. The fourth was a survivor who was accepted into the program within three months of the murder and was highly religious. She displayed feelings of great abandonment by all her support systems. She continued to seek a realignment with her church teachings which were unfulfilled. The Grief Experience Inventory testing confirmed the observations of little to no change for these two clients who completed the treatment program.

The group members are evaluated in individual progress reports on completion of the four tasks as outlined by Worden (1982), with description of the subsequent reorganization suggested by Davidson (1979).

Four criteria for reorganization are:

A.   A sense of release from the loss of the loved one.

B.   Renewed bursts of energy that can be confirmed by observers.

C.   Ability to make judgements and handle complex problems.

D.   A return to eating and sleeping habits previously experienced.

Many group members direct their energies and renewed problem solving abilities to changes in employment, seeking places of employment which are less demanding, less stressful, or more understanding of the need for time away for trial proceedings. This can more easily be arranged and contracted for at time of employment interviews. One member returned to where she had worked at the time of her daughter's murder with a renewed ability to challenge the employer's lack of understanding. Two professional men chose to move, feeling they could now put the murder behind them. Each expressed the desire for a new beginning. Both gained employment at higher levels in executive positions. One member held a meeting with her co-workers and employer to explain the process of grief and her need for support and acknowledgment. One member returned to school to become a pastor and plans to teach clergy how to care for victims of crime through seminars and presentations in local churches, national workshops, and bible colleges. She is an outstanding example that reaffirmation of religious beliefs is possible after the completion of one's own grief work. In her words, ''Grief work must come first. The church could not give me what I needed, but after the group (treatment program), I could return to the church and believe in God again!'' (And, do His work)!

Many group members direct energies to renewal of their marital relationship, reunite with families at gatherings, entertain in their own homes for the first time, complete long-awaited travel plans, or move to other areas. These activities are confirmed by onlookers and indicative of reorganization.

A member writing a self-help book, by her own admission, came to the group for further insight into the lives of other survivors for her book. At the screening intake session it was evident she had unresolved grief which she was trying to resolve through her writing. Writing is an excellent form of therapy, but unless directed to confrontive issues may not resolve the issues in the relationship. At the end of the second session, she released her resistance to being a group member and began to work earnestly on her own grief. She wrote the following passage and presented it with a gift at her final group session:

> ''The gift seems so trite in the realm of what you have given me, given us. What do you give to someone who has given you your life back? That has given two children their mother back? That has given a man his wife back? That has given

a mother a whole daughter back? What do you give a person who has performed the seemingly impossible? . . . In comparison I can give you nothing, absolutely nothing of comparable value. How much is my life worth? My husband would like to give you everything, my children thank you for their future, and I? I thank you for your compassion and the deep rooted need to help a sorrowful, crushed lot of people. . . .''

Prior to therapy the author quoted above had been suicidal. Her family life was disrupted. She had been to a psychologist who was not helpful due to lack of relevant knowledge. Imagine the pain that could have been prevented if the program could have been started earlier.

The group members provide a mirror reflection to one another which normalizes the symptoms. They provide support, and encourage one another. The therapist is the guide to direct, confront, challenge, and lead the group. The strength is in the group of survivors, not in the therapist. As a therapist your goal is to empower the survivors. When you provide a service as badly needed as this treatment program, the appreciation is most rewarding. However, the significant work has been accomplished by the group, not the leader.

The practitioner may use any therapeutic techniques which are familiar and comfortable in termination of the group. In the pilot project, time was spent in discussion of how to proceed beyond the pilot program to reach thousands of others whom are known to be in need of services. The group members' willingness to share their stories with others by providing a release for this educational material was directed toward that goal. This book has been written as one step toward this objective.

The professional may find that a great deal more time and effort must be expended toward community awareness of the needs that exist for homicide survivors, and in fund raising, than in provision of clinical skills.

Those who are certified in bereavement therapy will have no difficulty in training psychotherapists in the necessary clinical skills. The eight clinical interns trained in the HSGP program were eager to learn. All but one expressed lack of time to absorb the amount of materials necessary for the training. One, a thanatologist social worker, who had done extensive death education previously, was more familiar with the materials and found it easier to apply the principles of grief therapy to a group setting. The other trainees were shocked at the mental torment described by group members at intake sessions. Each contributed to their respective groups as they acknowledged the normal cognitive and affective behaviors due to the psychological trauma of this severity. Evaluations of the training course have been very positive. The clinical trainees are provided an individual evaluative session with the group leader.

Following the last session, our groups invite family members and concerned friends to meet with them to celebrate. There is a great deal of warmth, affection and congratulatory comments as the members applaud one another's efforts and progress. For the invited guests looking at *"THE GROUP,"* it may be difficult to remember the serious purpose that brought us into one another's lives. It is a very joyous occasion.

EVALUATIONS

Grief Experience Inventory

The pre-test and post-test have been administered to 43 homicide survivors in four separate groups. When first testing with this instrument the group members were given the pre-test to take home to complete following the intake session, and prior to the first group session. In 11 cases the test was either not turned in or not returned until later in the group therapy treatment program. The scores from those cases were eliminated as invalid. To prevent this complication pre-testing and post-testing are now a part of the respective First and Twelfth Sessions.

Comparison of scores on the pre-test and post-test of the Grief Experience Inventory (GEI) were completed in the remaining 32 cases. Testing for validity eliminated four additional cases. The scores for denial, atypical responses, and social desirability were scored above 70. Sanders (1979, p.5) states, "Sharing one's inner world of loss is difficult, even if the person is sincerely trying to be honest in order to advance the understanding of the bereavement process. People have cultural, religious, and familial models of how they should grieve. Their responses to test items could reflect more of how they think they should feel rather than their actual emotions."

The following changes were noted in the remaining sample population of n=28:

ITEM	IMPROVED	NO CHANGE	DECLINED
* Despair	20 = 71.4%	4 = 14.2%	4 = 14.2%
* Anger	18 = 64.2%	7 = 25 %	3 = 10.7%
* Guilt	18 = 64.2%	7 = 27 %	3 = 10.7%
Social Isolation	15 = 53.5%	8 = 28.5%	5 = 17.8%
Loss of Control	12 = 42.8%	12 = 42.8%	4 = 14.2%
Rumination	16 = 57.1%	7 = 25 %	5 = 17.8%
* Depersonalization	17 = 60.7%	8 = 28.5%	3 = 10.7%
* Somatization	22 = 78.5%	2 = 7.1%	4 = 14.2%
Death Anxiety	12 = 42.8%	10 = 35.7%	6 = 21.4%

(Does not equal 100%)

Discussion of Results:

There is marked improvement in 78.5% (22 of 28) in the area of physical symptoms. The areas of despair, anger, guilt, and depersonalization categories show impressive improvement for the majority of group members.

This graph does not reveal the degree of improvement. Many members begin the group program ranging in the 98 percentile scales in despair and complete the program with scores in the 2-5 percentile scales. Equally positive results are shown in the anger, guilt, depersonalization, and somatization scales.

The persons that scored less change or declined in each of these groups had the one common characteristic of being overtly religious who appeared to feel more betrayed by their belief system. There is great difficulty in resolution of the death when one feels betrayed by deeply held beliefs.

The increase in rumination and death anxiety may be attributed to the constant homework assignments and facing the reality of death. These phenomena are prevalent and expected when proceeding through focused grief work. The five members who tested higher in social isolation revealed the lack of an outside support system. It could be suggested that during group these members were receiving more support than previously. However, because the members are witnessing marked support for other members from families and friends, they are more aware of their own lack of acknowledgment by outside others.

Those who scored greater on the loss of control variable after the group treatment program, scored the most improved in relief of guilt feelings. This may indicate they were able to give up the feelings of being responsible so felt less guilty, but, in accepting the inactivation brought on by the murder and the courts, felt an increased sense of loss of control.

It is interesting to note the one person selected in each group as "most improved" by the respective group, was also the one who scored most improvement in the GEI, in each of the four groups. There appears to be a positive correlation between the subjective and objective measurements of progress.

Subjective measurements of the Group Grief Therapy Treatment Program are very positive. The objective measurements as translated by the GEI scores indicate improvement for the majority of members. The sample is small for translation to a large homicide survivor population at this time, however, conclusions may be valid for a trend analysis.

Therapists under contract to HSGP are requested to use the GEI pre- and post-test with the groups they lead. Anyone who leads a group from the design in this text is invited to share results of GEI testing with the author. Objective testing is essential. As professionals, we must constantly evaluate the results of our work to insure continued improvement and test for desired outcome.

Evaluation by Professionals in Clinical Training

Evaluative statements from group co-leaders were positive and constructive. The following are quotes made by clinical trainees in the role of group co-leader:

1. "There is no doubt, based upon my clinical assessment, that the project provided grief therapy to the homicide survivors through the extremely well designed group treatment format. Given the severe bereavement reactions which were displayed in all except the newly widowed client (too recently into survivorhood for a pattern to have developed), the group was more effective, hence more economically valid than any method I have seen in over ten years of thanatological study and clinical work."

2. "I have found that I now feel aware of the specific areas which are unique to homicide survivors and some methods which will definitely help them work through their grief so that their lives are touched in a positive manner in spite of the horrific loss they have experienced."

3. "The equity with which the therapists were treated, the organization of the group sessions, and the extensive readings all lend to a course of study for professional therapists to acquire the ability to work with homicide survivors in groups. The course of study and the mode, i.e., a tremendous amount of reading material related in a timely manner to the topics of the groups, as well as the fairly non-directive teaching approach were all positive from a course standpoint."

4. "Although there were many similarities between some of my Vietnam veterans and their experiences as survivors, there was also the homicide specific items and these allowed me to gain in general knowledge. The survivors were the real teachers, as they should always be, and from them came a certain amount of humility as well — it was an honor to experience the group process with them."

5. "The boundaries of thanatology are not the limiting usefulness of the course."

Note:
In this regard, one therapist has used the course work redesigned for the elderly in a group treatment home; and has successfully completed two groups in that setting. Another therapist used the course work to enhance adolescent group work with hospitalized adolescents and reports positive results. A third clinical trainee has translated the course of therapy to a suicide survivors group which she leads. Three therapists have become available for individual homicide survivor case referrals. One other therapist, who was provided training, moved into a supervisory position and has been unable to participate in further clinical work. One trainee is no longer employed by the participating mental health agency.

6. "It seems that criteria for therapist selection are valid, that those with previous thanatological experience will have the greater likelihood of being able to integrate the readings, group experience, and the discussion and teaching aspects."

7. "Due to the frequent turnover of agency personnel . . . those selected should be licensed to practice. . . Contracts with individuals seem better than contracts with agencies. If we view knowledge as dynamic and ever building, then the continuity of the therapists is also critical to refining the model. I remain somewhat dazzled by the effectiveness of this method, but the theoretical underpinnings are such that it could be predicted to be effective."

8. "A course workbook will be useful, but then establishment of a more predictable outline will also result in the teacher being less of a creative obstacle to learning than at present."

It is of the gravest concern to the author, that there is no "how-to book" that can do justice to meeting the unique individual needs of survivors of homicide. Each professional must rely on the ability to be flexible and recognize the individuality in each and every life. One's ability to truly care will do much to enhance this work. It is a challenge to conduct a time-limited therapy group and gain the marked improvements possible in this population. I hope this text will encourage mental health professionals to meet this challenge.

Consultive services on individual cases or to establish a program are available from the author.

FINAL GROUP EVALUATION

GROUP MEMBERS: You have completed a course of Group Grief Therapy for Homicide Survivors. The 12 sessions offered have been directed at helping to resolve your grief for your murdered loved one. Please complete this evaluation so we may be better able to meet the needs of others who may come after you.

1. I have attended _____ sessions.

2. The sessions which I personally gained the most from were: (circle)

   (1)-(2) My Grief (3) My Relationship with the Deceased
   (4) Anger (5) Guilt (6)-(7) Relationship with my Family
   (8) Ambivalence (9) Funerals (10) Memorials
   (11) Unfinished Business (12) Final

3. The session least helpful for me was _____.
   (Use number above)

4. If *you* had the opportunity to join this group at any time since the murder, in your own experience would it have been more helpful: (circle)

   3-6 months after;   7-12 months after;   2 years after;   3 years;   other;

5. Each session of 2 hours seems: (circle)

   the right amount of time;   too long;   not enough time.

6. I (have) (have not) been able to do the homework assignments.

   completed some   completed most   completed all   completed none

7. Please make any other comments which you feel would be helpful on:

   Scheduling:

   Therapists:

   Locations:

   Setting:

   Other:

Thank you for your time and effort to make this project possible.

HOMICIDE SURVIVORS THERAPY GROUP

Final Evaluation for Therapists in Training

1.   This project was designed to meet three major objectives.

    A.   To provide grief therapy to homicide survivors through use of the group process.

    B.   To train two psychotherapists in the education and clinical skills of grief therapy for use with homicide survivors.

    C.   To develop a course of study to train facilitators and group leaders for homicide survivor therapy groups.

    Please address each objective and evaluate the level each was met. In your experience, if the objective was not met, what prevented the goal from being reached?

2.   Each therapist had personal and professional goals. Evaluate your own goals. To what level were they met? If not, reasons you think they were not attained?

3.   Each agency that provides therapists to be trained has agency requirements. HSGP has established criteria for selection of therapists. In your experience, what effect did this have on your educational and skills development? Do you think it enhances the training/ teaching/educational process when the criteria are used? If not, state reasons. Should the criteria be changed to meet the needs of each agency and, if so, how?

    Criteria for selection of therapists:

    A.   Based on interview and qualifications those therapists who volunteer to learn death related counseling skills useful with homicide survivors.

    B.   Previous death education courses; membership in a thanatology organization; attendance in four or more workshops in thanatology; previous commitment and interest in any other death related interest area, i.e., terminal illness, children's death, suicide.

    C.   To meet the needs of the victim advocates who are employed by the law enforcement and criminal justice system offices for a referral source, those applicants who by position or title work with adults will be given priority.

    Please make any other comments you think will be useful for the project. Thank you for your commitment and interest!

APPENDIX A

HOMICIDE SURVIVORS GROUP
INTAKE FORM

I.   IDENTIFYING INFORMATION:

    1. Name: _____ Intake Date: _____

    2. Address: _____
                           (City, State & Zip)

    3. Phone No.: _____ _____ D.O.B.: _____
                  (Home)   (Work)

    4. Referred by: _____

II.   INFORMATION REGARDING THE DECEASED:

    1. Name & Age of Deceased: _____

    2. Relationship to Deceased: _____

    3. Date of Death: _____D.O.B.: _____

    4. Age of Applicant at Date of Death of Deceased: _____

    5. Circumstances of Death: _____

6. Status of Murderer:

7. Court Experience:

Depositions:

Hearings:

Personal Testimony:

Trials:

Appeals:

Other:

III.   ROLES/FUNCTIONAL LEVELS:

1. Role/Functional Level of Deceased:

2. Role/Functional Level of Survivor Prior to the Death:

3. Present Role/Functioning of Survivor (use applicant's own words):

4. Meaning of the Loss:

5. Relationship with Deceased (dependent, nurturing, ambivalent, satisfying, etc.):

6. Previous and Present Coping Skills:

	Previous	Present
A. Avoidance of painful stimuli		
B. Distraction		
C. Drugs, alcohol, food		
D. Rumination		
E. Impulsive		
F. Prayer		
G. Rationalization/intellectualization		
H. Avoidance/contact with people		

7. Past Mental Health History:

8. Present Mental Health:

   A. Emotional state:

   B. Suicidal ideation:

   C. Eating patterns:

   D. Sleep patterns:

   E. Health problems:

   F. Date of last physical examination; results:

   G. Exercise:

   H. Use of drugs and sedatives:

   I. Maturity and intelligence level:

9. Past Experiences with Death/Loss:

IV. SOCIAL/CULTURAL/ETHNIC/RELIGIOUS AFFILIATION:

1. Describe (i.e., Italian; Catholic; 2nd generation raised in U.S./Strong Greek heritage; Greek-speaking parents; Greek Orthodox Church; church attendance, etc.):

2. Sex Role Conditioning:

3. Timeliness of Death:

4. Perception of Preventability:

5. Secondary Losses:

6. Concurrent Stressors:

V. SOCIAL SUPPORT SYSTEM:

1. Available:

2. Ability to Reach Out for Support:

3. Educational Status:

4. Economic Status:

5. Occupational Status:

6. Funeral Rituals for Deceased:

VI.   FAMILY SYSTEM: (Provide structure in genogram)

VII. IMPRESSION:

APPENDIX B

RELEASE FORM

The Homicide Survivors Group of Pinellas County is a pilot project sponsored by the West Coast Florida Chapter of the Association for Death Education and Counseling, Inc., the Pinellas County Sheriff's Department and the Mental Health Services of Upper Pinellas. One of the objectives of this project is to train and educate mental health professionals to work with and support homicide survivors. To meet this objective, an educational film will be produced by Lula M. Redmond, R.N., M.S., LMFT, Clinical Director and Trainer for the project.

The film will be used in national training workshops directed to an audience of psychiatrists, psychologists, social workers, nurses, funeral directors, physicians, legislators, mental health professionals, law enforcement staff, victim advocates, and others seeking training and information in death education and counseling.

In order that they may learn what has been helpful in this program, I give permission to film sessions which I attend and use the information documented for the express purpose of producing an educational film.

_____   _____

Signature   Date

_____   _____

Signature   Date

APPENDIX C

REQUIREMENTS FOR THERAPISTS IN TRAINING

Required Reading: To be read and discussed with instructor prior to intakes of homicide survivors.

Rando, Therese A., (1984) *Grief, Dying, And Death; Clinical Interventions for Caregivers,* Research Press, Champaign IL.

Worden, J. William, (1982) *Grief Counseling and Grief Therapy, A Handbook for the Mental Health Practitioner,* Springer Publishing Co.

van der Kolk, Bessel A., (1987) *Psychological Trauma,* The Role of the Group in the Origin and Resolution of the Trauma Response, p. 153-171, American Psychiatric Press, Washington, D.C. 1987.

Clinical therapists in training as co-leaders in the Group Grief Therapy Program are required to complete each assignment in preparation for the subsequent session of grief therapy. All discussion questions are taken from these assignments.

Session I: Bowen, Murray, (1976) *"Family Reaction to Death,"* Family Therapy, Theory and Practice, p. 335-348, ed. Philip J. Guerin, Gardner Press, Inc.

Session II: Wass, Hannelore, ed. (1979) *Dying: Facing The Facts,* Hemisphere Publishing Corporation; Edgar N. Jackson, "Bereavement and Grief, p. 256-28l; Glen W. Davidson, "Mourning Process Not Understood" p. 173-180.

Session III: Feifel, Herman, (1977) *New Meanings of Death,* McGraw-Hill Book Company; Robert J. Lifton, "The Sense of Immortality: On Death And The Continuity of Life," p. 274-289.

Rando, Therese A., (1988) *Grieving: How To Go On Living When Someone You Love Dies,* p. 89-106, Lexington, Mass.

Session IV: van der Kolk, Bessel A., (1984) *Post-Traumatic Stress Disorder: Psychological and Biological Sequelae,* American Psychiatric Press.

Review: *Diagnostic and Statistical Manual of Mental Disorders,* 3rd ed. (1987), classification 309.8; Post Traumatic Stress Disorder, Chronic or Delayed American Psychiatric Association, Washington, D.C.

Session V: Lifton, Robert J., (1979) *The Broken Connection: On Death And The Continuity Of Life,* "Anger, Rage, and Violence," p. 147-162; "Survivor Experience and Traumatic Syndrome," p. 163-178, Simon and Schuster, New York.

Hankins, Gary, (1988) *Prescriptions For Anger: Coping With Angry Feelings and Angry People,* Princess Pub., OR.

Session VI: Complete evaluations on Course of Study, Group Process, Self-Evaluation, and Instructor. Print or type.

Session VII: Ramsay, Ronald W. and Noorbergen, Rene, (1981) *Living With Loss: A Dramatic New Breakthrough in Grief Therapy,* William Morrow and Company, New York.

Session VIII: Rando, Therese A., (1984) *Grief, Dying, And Death: Clinical Interventions for Caregivers,* "Funerals and Funerary Rituals," p. 173-197.

Session IX: Morgan, Ernest, (1984) *A Manual of Death Education and Simple Burial,* Celo Press, N.C., Review Appendix VIII, "Sample Death Ceremonies," p. 122-142.

Volkan, Vamik D., (1981) *Linking Objects and Linking Phenomena: A Study of the Forms, Symptoms, Metapsychology, and Therapy of Complicated Mourning,* p. 1- 154; "Re-Grief Therapy" p. 201-233, International Universities Press, Inc. New York.

Session X: Prepare evaluations for group members.

Osterweis, Marian, Fredric Solomon, and Morris Green, eds, (1984) *Bereavement Reactions, Consequences and Care,* "Adult's Reaction to Bereavement" p. 47-68; "Reactions to Particular Types of Bereavement" p. 71-95; "Bereavement Intervention Programs" p. 239-277, National Academy Press, Washington, D.C.

Session XI: Knapp, Ronald J., (1986) *Beyond Endurance, When A Child Dies,* Schocken Books, New York.

Rando, Therese A., (1986) *Parental Loss Of A Child,* p. 5-119; p. 341-413, Research Press, Champaign, IL.

Session XII: Review evaluations from group members. Collate and examine for patterns. Note similarities and differences. Suggest recommendations.

Arrange to review filming and audio recordings. Schedule interview with instructor for evaluations.

Prepare for next group using evaluative summaries as guides.

APPENDIX D

HOMICIDE SURVIVORS THERAPY GROUP

STUDY QUESTIONS:

1. Complete Self-Awareness exercise. Turn in prior to Session I.

2. Write out your professional and personal objectives for this training. What are your objectives for the group members?

3. In what ways might the "emotional shockwave" as described by Bowen manifest itself in family members of homicide?

4. What grief reactions might be expressed by an emotionally cutoff member?

5. In what ways does the functional level of the deceased and the dependency level of the survivor affect the grief process?

6. Compare this experience in the initial session with homicide survivors to previous experience with groups of survivors from other causes of death. How do these differ? What similarities are apparent? What preparation would assist the therapist to work with this client population? (questions 2,3,4,5,6 due Session II)

7. Write out normal grief reactions and symptomatology of bereaved survivors.

8. Compare and contrast Therese Rando's grief assessment; Catherine Sander's, "Bereavement Typologies and Implications for Therapy," and Bowlby and Parke's descriptions of the mourning process.

9. Write out William Worden's four tasks of mourning, and what the griever experiences during each task. What therapeutic interventions might be helpful throughout the process? What might indicate the survivor is unable to complete each task? (questions 7,8,9 due Session III)

10. Write out definitions for the intrapsychic processes of introjection and identification.

11. What are the five modes of symbolic immortality as conceptualized by Robert J. Lifton? Name and describe each.

12. What effect would murder (sudden violent death) have on survivors in relation to Lifton's modes of immortality? In what way does this differ from expected deaths? (questions 10,11,12 due Session IV)

13. What similarities and differences can you identify in the group members using the PTSD classification in DSM III? Write out for each group member.

14. What parallel behaviors can you identify in the group members using the PTSD classification in DSM III? Write out for each group member. (questions 13,14 due Session V)

15. List and describe ten expressions of anger that have a therapeutic effect.

16. How does the expression of anger have a therapeutic effect? What kinds of expressions need to be avoided?

17. Lifton outlines a three stage process for a survivor of a traumatic situation in "Emancipation From the Bondage of his Own Inner Deadness." Address each stage in order. How has our work with survivors of homicide followed that process? If not, what process do you identify?

18. In what way do the concepts that Hankins describes apply to the psychological trauma experienced by homicide survivors? At what point do you think Hankins' concepts would be most useful? (questions 15,16,17,18 due Session VI)

19. Complete evaluations on course, group process, self-evaluation, and instructor. (due Session VII)

20. How do the methods used in Guided Confrontation Therapy compare to Grief Therapy presently used with the group? Note similarities and differences. (due Session VIII)

21. What are the purposes of funerals in our society?

22. Address the difficulties survivors of murder experience during funerals. Consider identification of the deceased, delays due to a coroner's examination, emotional state, crisis intervention theory, intrusion by other systems, grief theory, anxious systems, and value of funerals and rituals. (questions 21,22 due Session IX)

23. What is the value of a memorial service in honor of a deceased loved one?

24. Describe "Re-Grief" Therapy as practiced by Vamik D. Volkan, M.D.

25. What is a linking object? In what way can you, as the therapist, assist the client in decathexis by use of the linking object? (questions 23,24,25 due Session X)

26. Prepare evaluations for the group.

27. What is your conceptualization of an adult's reaction to bereavement? Note the differences for particular types of death. (questions 26,27 due Session XI)

28. Based on your knowledge of Bereavement Intervention Programs, formulate and address three research questions, i.e., what research is needed to design effective programs?

29. Address difficulties of the parental loss of a child. Compare this to other losses studied. (questions 28,29 due Session XII)

30. Complete evaluations. Compare your objectives for course of study and clinical training, personal and professional goals with objectives prior to course.

APPENDIX E

First Proposal   9/85

HOMICIDE SURVIVORS GROUP INC. OF PINELLAS COUNTY

Statement of Purpose

We propose to provide a Group Grief Therapy Treatment Program with a component of a peer mutual support group under professional leadership for the victim survivors of homicidal deaths in Pinellas County.

Criteria for development of the group includes:

1.   Networking of community agencies to establish need, continuity and direction.

2.   Provision of quality death education and bereavement counseling skills for the mental health professionals who lead the group.

3.   Must be provided in a recognized community agency in a therapeutic setting for the survivors.

The supporting agencies have assessed the need and have collective experiences to support and document this as an unmet need of the homicide survivor. A therapy program and peer mutual support group under professional leadership can be provided at the most reasonable cost for the numbers to be served.

Supporting Agencies

The West Coast Florida Chapter of the Association For Death Education and Counseling, Inc. This is a local chapter of a national organization that provides educational programs, trains and certifies expertise in the field of Thanatology, promotes and upgrades the quality of death education in educational institutions at all levels, and is directed to upgrade the quality of counseling in the areas of death, dying, and bereavement. The founding member of the local chapter, Lula M. Redmond, R.N., M.S.,LMFT, is a family therapist in private practice who specializes in unresolved grief, and is nationally certified as a Death Educator and a Bereavement Counselor, will direct the formation of the group and train two co-therapists for each group formed for homicide survivors.

Victim Advocacy Program of the Pinellas County Sheriff's Department

This program under the leadership of Sara Sopkin, Senior Victim Advocate, provides crisis intervention assistance at the time of notification of next of kin; assesses the immediate needs of the victim survivors; assist the survivors throughout the criminal justice system; serves as liaison for the victims with law enforcement, courts, and corrections; and makes appropriate referrals to community agencies. It is this agency who first defined the need for an educationally sound, therapeutic support group to meet the emotional needs of the victim survivors. This program will assist by making appropriate referrals based on assessed needs of the victim survivors both at the time of death, and during crisis periods experienced during prolonged court dates.

Mental Health Services of Upper Pinellas, Inc.

This is an established private non-profit community mental health center. Staff members include psychiatrists, psychologists, social workers and other mental health professionals trained in providing specific therapeutic services to children, adults and senior adults. MHSUP will assist in the screening and intake of individual members, provide therapists to be trained as co-leaders with the group, provide physical setting for meeting space, and provide printing and mailing services when necessary.

All three agencies are in prime situations to refer clients in need of the service to the group.

Statement of Need

Bereaved survivors experience a complexity of physical illness, emotional turmoil and social changes regardless of the cause of the death of their loved one. Conflicts imposed on the survivor must be resolved in order for life to be productive and livable. Changes in the status and role of parents affects their home and work life as the mind is filled with longing, aching pain of a future without their child. Widows and widowers need to learn new roles, establish a new identity and develop new and oftentimes different goals for their life without a partner. Children who survive the death of their siblings or parents are often lost in a void and meaningless world. Physical symptoms of insomnia, inability to eat, heartache, restlessness, muscle tension, and a heavy weight in the chest predominate. Emotions of anger, remorse, guilt, fear, sudden unexpected crying, and nightmares, become frightening to a person who has controlled his behavior previously. Loss of concentration and disorganization at work begins to lead to poor work performance, productivity decreases and may lead to loss of employment. Frequent use of alcohol or other drug abuse may occur, used as a sedative to relieve the pain. Children may lash out in uncontrollable angry behaviors, miss school, fail courses even when identified as a bright or gifted student, lash out at friends and teachers, or withdraw from everyone to nurse the raw open wound of *GRIEF.*

These behaviors, thoughts, and feelings increase dramatically for the survivor of a homicide. We must understand the meaning of death to accept it. The homicidal death usually cannot be explained in terms of our value and belief systems. Our belief is in a fair society. Homicide survivors must not only deal with the raw painful reality of grief but be confronted with media, press, law enforcement officials, and a legal system which is unfamiliar and a painfully slow process.

The Harvard Bereavement Study and the recent Presidential Commission on the Study of Bereavement clearly document the increased mortality and morbidity rates for survivors.

Intervention, either on an individual basis or in group therapy, can alter the course and halt the disruptive cycle of a prolonged and exaggerated grief reaction.

Employers, teachers, clergy, physicians, professionals in all areas are only too familiar with the subsequent loss of a productive life as seen in their employees, students, and clients following the death of a beloved family member.

Presently in Pinellas County, despite the high rate of homicides, there is no identified service center to provide the much needed psychological support required by the homicide survivor.

No funding is provided for psychological counseling and many victim survivors cannot afford this service to regain emotional stability and prevent long term disability. Further, resentment is registered by the survivor who cannot accept that he must pay for counseling at a time when there was no decision, no choice that he become a survivor. It becomes acceptable to relate to the only other people who understand, other homicide survivors.

Population At Risk

In 1984, fifty homicides were prosecuted in Pinellas County. This does not count those crimes in which no suspect was arrested.

Immediate family members, parents, children, spouses, grandparents, and close relatives who are directly involved with the death and resulting grief reaction average seven to ten members per family. These figures are based on the writer's private practice experience in which one member up to 16 family members may be seen in counseling. This indicates that from the year 1984 alone, we have 400-500 persons swallowed up in the depths of emotional turmoil and confusion following the murder of their loved one. Add to that those who are recent survivors and those whose loved one was murdered two to three years earlier and we realize our numbers are astronomic!

(In a short T.V. interview last week, the writer was only asked one question by the T.V. reporter, which describes the longevity of the pain. He asked, "Does the bitterness ever stop?" His sister was murdered eight years ago!)

Resources/Funding

We have described the three agencies which will provide the referrals. We possess the educational expertise and counseling skills to provide the service. We are willing to expend the time, energy and manpower to assess the individuals, screen for appropriateness, design and implement the treatment program. We have a selected site mid-county which will offer the services in a convenient location to the majority of clients. We have the goodwill and moral support of many community agencies. But we do not have necessary funding to begin the service.

As a combined effort we are requesting funds to begin two groups, each group to run 12 weeks in 2 hour sessions, meeting once a week for 12-15 survivors per group. Subsequent funding will be requested from the National Institute of Mental Health, and other state and national agencies following this initial project.

APPENDIX F

Second Proposal   11/86

HOMICIDE SURVIVORS GROUP INC. OF PINELLAS COUNTY

STATEMENT OF PURPOSE

We propose to provide a Grief Therapy Treatment Program and mutual support group under professional leadership for the victim survivors of homicidal deaths in Pinellas County. Criteria for development of the group includes:

1.   Networking of community agencies to establish need, continuity, and direction.

2.   Provision of quality death education and bereavement counseling skills for the mental health professionals who lead the group.

3.   Presentation in a recognized community agency in a therapeutic setting for the survivors.

The supporting agencies have assessed the need and have collective experiences to support and document this as an unmet need of the homicide survivor. A treatment program and mutual peer support group under professional leadership can be provided at the most reasonable cost for the greatest numbers to be served.

INTRODUCTION

A Homicide Survivors Therapy Group has been successfully developed for Pinellas County in Clearwater, Florida. The first group tested as a pilot project has been developed by Lula M. Redmond, R.N., M.S., LMFT, with the cooperation of the Victim Advocacy Program of the Pinellas County Sheriff's Department and the Mental Health Services of Upper Pinellas. The pilot project had the following objectives defined:

1.   To provide grief therapy in a group setting to family members who have experienced the murder of one of its members. The murder of a loved one creates a wide range of psychological trauma for the survivors.

2.   To train two psychotherapists in grief therapy for homicide survivors from each local community agency. Clinical skills training to be provided as therapist accepts the role of co-leaders of the group. The therapist, after training, would be qualified to accept referrals of homicide survivors for counseling in their respective agency.

3.   To develop a course of study for the training of psychotherapists who could lead Homicide Survivors Therapy Groups.

The first two objectives have been attained. The third objective will require the subsequent completion of two additional groups to test the study course.

This would not have been achieved without the generous financial support of the Junior League of St. Petersburg, Inc. and the League of Victim and Emphathizers (LOVE) Group of Palm Harbor. Both organizations have provided support, made referrals to the Homicide Survivors Group, and are to be commended for their caring concerns for the people of our community!

STATEMENT OF NEED

Bereaved survivors experience a complexity of physical illness, emotional turmoil and social changes regardless of the cause of death of a family member. Conflicts imposed on the survivor due to death of a loved one must be resolved in order for future life to be productive.

Changes in the status and role of parents affect their home and work life as the mind is filled with the longing, aching pain of a future without their child. Widows and widowers find they need to learn new and different roles, establish a new identity and develop goals for a life without a partner. Children who survive their sibling or parents death are often lost in an emotional void and unrelating world.

Physical symptoms of insomnia, loss of appetite, heartache, stress, restlessness, muscle tension, and somatization predominate. Emotions of anger, remorse, guilt, fear, sudden unexpected crying, and nightmares, become frightening to the person who has lost such control.

Loss of concentration and disorganization begin to lead to poor work performance, productivity decreases and may lead to loss of employment. Alcohol and drugs may be used to relieve the pain, sometimes leading to addiction.

Children may lash out at friends and teachers in uncontrollable angry behaviors, miss school, fail courses even when identified as a bright or gifted student. Also, they may withdraw from everyone to nurse the raw open wound of *GRIEF.*

These behaviors, thoughts, and feelings increase dramatically for the survivor of a homicide. We must understand the meaning of death to be able to accept it. It is more difficult to understand the intentional act of killing a human being, oftentimes an innocent child or elderly person. The homicidal death cannot be explained in terms of our value and belief system. We have been taught to believe in a fair society. Nothing in life prepares survivors for the day when a loved one is murdered. The dimension of cruelty compounds the sense of sorrow and loss with acute feelings of injustice, distrust, powerlessness, hopelessness, depression, and helplessness. The grief reactions, which are normal, may have to be delayed while the survivor confronts the media, press, law enforcement officials, and a legal system which is unfamiliar, painfully complicated, and slow moving.

The Harvard Bereavement Study and the recent Presidential Commission on the Study of Bereavement clearly document the increased mortality and morbidity rates for survivors. Intervention, either on an individual basis or in group therapy, can alter the course and halt the disruptive cycle of a prolonged and exaggerated grief reaction.

Until the pilot program, Homicide Survivors Therapy Group in Pinellas County, was organized there was no identified service center to provide the much needed psychological care required by homicide survivors.

Funding that was provided by the Junior League of St. Petersburg, Inc. and the LOVE Group have made the pilot project possible. There are no accessible funds for psychological counseling for homicide survivors. Many victim survivors cannot afford mental health services to regain emotional stability or to prevent long term disability.

Further, the survivor resents charges for the service of counseling when there was no choice, no decision made that he become a survivor of a murder victim. It becomes acceptable and therapeutic to relate to the only other people who can truly understand, others whose loved one also was murdered.

These following comments were made by members of the Homicide Survivors Group after therapy in the pilot project. These reveal a sense of release from the emotional turmoil survivors had been experiencing:

"I feel this group has started to bring me back to the world of the living after 18 months of pure *HELL*. If called on, I will do whatever is necessary to see this program continued and that is a promise."(Mother, 54: son, 24, knifed to death 18 months ago).

"The Homicide Survivors Group has been a tearful but positive learning experience for me. This group has reached a part of me that has been secluded since my father's murder. A part of me that was locked away by the murderer has now been opened by me, with the support and guidance of the group. My thanks are endless!" (Daughter, 28: father, 52, murdered 10 years ago).

"I don't feel alone anymore. I will get more control of things with this process. My Rabbi did not know about *MURDER*. This group has done more than anyone. In the last three weeks I can see a whole new way of life for me." (Son, 43: father brutally beaten, murdered 11 years ago).

"In the last three weeks, it's like I've suddenly walked out into a clearing. The woods are behind me now." (Daughter, 29: father, 52, murdered 3 years ago).

"Murder is something that must be dealt with now, not two (to 11) years from now as is the case of some of the people in the group. Money must be made available to offer help soon after the crime is committed. Years of mental stress can lead to other problems. A survivor never really leaves all things behind, but the sooner a survivor can get on with life the better. Murder is not planned by the survivors, you don't put pennies away for a rainy day to pay for therapy, thus financial help must come in the way of funding. Perhaps a way of obtaining this money is to 'hit up' the murderer's social security fund. Transfer these earnings into a general fund to help with therapy for the survivors." (Mother, 50: victim, daughter 25; then murderer committed suicide).

"I feel very fortunate to have found this group. During the first year after my mother's murder, I tried contacting several different places for guidance and was told none existed...This type of therapy is greatly needed for there are a great amount of surviving victims in our society today, unfortunately, not receiving any help.

"I must make mention that since being in the therapy group..., my biggest relief has been finding out that I am normal. A lot of us feel that we are losing control of ourselves and that in itself is very frightening.

Also, even though the sessions are sometimes painful and difficult to attend, I have found that I am finding myself in better moods during the week that follows each meeting. I think that is because we are dealing with our feelings openly and honestly, that I'm not carrying it around constantly as before, therefore I am getting my old self back and starting to enjoy life once again. I feel this is a result of the therapy group." (Daughter, 38: mother, 55, burglarized and murdered in her home by a 17 year old juvenile whose family was court ordered to move from another state 2 years ago).

Evaluation by Therapist

In Grief Therapy, one of the best measures in evaluating successful resolution is in actions and behaviors that are taken by the client, either during or following therapy. The actions may be reported by the client or visibly witnessed by others.

In the pilot project for the Homicide Survivors Group the clients reported the following actions they had taken by the midpoint of the 12 sessions during the therapy program.

"I have been able to finish unfinished business such as dealing with the police reports, and being able to go back home with a more positive attitude."

"Controlling my anger at my husband."

"Understanding that some of the things I felt very important such as the cause of the death on the death certificate of the murderer is not as important as it was in the beginning."

"Talking to my mother. Not covering up the truth to protect others. Talking more freely and honestly to my friends about my father's murder and how I miss him."

"Actively sifting through the events that I buried inside myself for three years. I'm actively engaged in my anger toward people who violated me during the early months after the murder."

"I am no longer surrogate father to my brothers and sisters."

"Courage to delve into the circumstances surrounding (my son's) death. Courage to tell someone not to burden me with their problems until I can solve my own."

The survivors presented a high level of disorganization and confusion at the screening intake sessions. Upon completion of the therapy treatment program, thinking processes became prioritized. Members were able to make positively focused decisions and take actions which appeared impossible twelve weeks earlier.

POPULATION AT RISK

In 1984, fifty homicides were prosecuted in Pinellas County. This does not count those murders in which no suspect was apprehended and arrested.

Immediate family members: parents, children, spouses, grandparents and close relatives directly involved with the murder and resulting grief reaction can average 7-10 members per family. As a Grief Therapist, I have had up to 16 family members in counseling after a murder.

In the pilot project Homicide Survivors Group, we have seven members and 58 other family members who have been discussed as friends, neighbors or others.

This indicates from the year 1984 alone, we have 400-500 persons swallowed up in the depths of emotional turmoil and confusion that follows the murder of a loved one. Add to that those who are recent survivors, those whose loved ones were murdered two to three years earlier, and those who have moved to this area, where the homicide is not recorded in Pinellas County. The figures are astronomically high and warrant immediate action!

RESOURCES/FUNDING

At a total cost of $3,600 for 10 members, the pilot project cost $360 per member or $30 per 2 hour group session per individual member. This compares favorably to individual counseling rates in our psychiatric community. Psychiatrists charge $110; psychologists $85-90; marriage and family therapist $75; and counselors $60 per hour.

The program will seek to enroll 10-12 members for the next group, to allow for the possibility of drop-outs and the higher cost factor. The group leader and two co-leaders are adequate to provide services for 10-12 members without reducing effectiveness.

The referral sources, educational expertise and counseling skills are adequate to provide quality services to homicide survivors. There is a willingness to expend the time, energy and manpower to organize and coordinate the group.

The Homicide Survivors Group has the interest, goodwill and moral support of many community agencies. The need exists for funds to begin another 12 week treatment program.

APPENDIX G

ORGANIZATIONAL PLAN

The Homicide Survivors Group, Inc. of Pinellas County will operate under the following guidelines.

SERVICES

1. A course of Group Grief Therapy will be provided by a licensed mental health professional; the group will number no more than 10 members per group; provide 12 sessions of 2 hours each session of psychotherapy.

2. All members cases will be reviewed with a licensed practicing psychiatrist who is knowledgeable about the grief process. Reviews may be accomplished in direct supervision with the physician and psychotherapist.

3. No more than two psychotherapists may be in training for one group. Each group leader will train an additional therapist through a clinical practicum in the group. Course work required outside the group must be accomplished prior to accepting the clinician as a trained provider of services.

4. Volunteers who have been trained in a 12 hour volunteer training course may be on call to respond to the needs of newly bereaved homicide survivors.

5. Individual counseling may be referred to any of the trained providers of service.

6. Identified homicide survivors who telephone for psychological assistance will be served by either a trained volunteer, a psychotherapist, or the physician.

7. Homicide survivors who request legal assistance will be referred to League of Victims and Empathizers, Inc.; or Justice For Surviving Victims, Inc. Legal issues will not be in the province of HSGP services.

REFERRAL NETWORK

1. The Victim Advocacy Program of the Pinellas County Sheriff's Office will refer families and friends of murdered victims to HSGP.

2. Mental health agencies and other public and private health organizations will be a source of referrals.

3. The Pinellas County Victim Rights Coalition members will be a source of referrals.

4. Victim Advocates from all county, state or government agencies and municipal police departments may refer to HSGP.

5.   Referrals will be acknowledged either by telephone or in writing, as is common practice in mental health services.

6.   All referrals will be logged in with date, request name, address, telephone number, and disposition of case.

7.   Evaluation at three months; six months; and twelve months following the completion of group grief therapy will be completed by a trained volunteer or the group leader of the client.

8.   When appropriate, individual counseling sessions will be provided at reduced fee schedules. History, intake information, and previous psychiatric treatment are known factors about this client; these factors lead to the greatest cost for the psychotherapist, therefore can be appropriately reduced.

SERVICE DELIVERY AREA

1.   Homicide survivors who live in Pinellas County will be provided service on a first-come, first-served basis.

2.   Survivors who request group admission from neighboring counties will be provided services when openings are available. No more than two members from other counties will be accepted in any one group. This will enhance outreach efforts to train additional psychotherapists in the future.

3.   The setting selected for the group meeting will be located in a public, easily accessible building. The names of identified mental health agencies connotes a mental illness is to be treated. Since grief is a normal reaction to loss, labeled mental health facilities will be avoided to prevent associated labeling of the survivors.

4.   Churches of any denomination will be avoided to prevent the connotation of a religious affiliation with a particular religious belief system.

FEE SCHEDULE

1.   Homicide survivors who request individual counseling prior to group intake will be charged the normal rate for psychological services.

2.   Survivors who apply for admission to the group will be charged $240.00 for the 12 week sessions, based on their ability to pay.

3.   Since additional financial constraints are precipitating to the family of a murder victim, the cost of providing services will be reduced for those unable to pay.

4.   Follow-up and individual services will be provided at reduced fees, as stated above.

FUNDING

1.   The program must be funded by outside resources if it is to be provided.

2.   Grant applications, bequests, private sector corporations, and other organizations will be asked to provide funding for the program.

3.   City, county, state and government grant applications will be submitted.

4.   Local and national service organizations will be requested to fund the HSGP.

5.   Funds from private donors will be accepted and acknowledged.

ACCOUNTING

1.   All monies that are received by HSGP from any and all sources will be accounted in the bookkeeping and accounting of income and expenses for HSGP.

2.   An annual audit will be performed by a reliable outside auditing firm. The audit will be available for review by any and all interested parties upon request.

3.   A checking and savings account will be opened by the operating officers in charge of the organization. Deposits may be made by the officers. Withdrawals will require the signature of the operating president or the treasurer, upon approval of the board.

4.   Fees paid to service delivery personnel will be approved by the Board of Directors.

5.   Accounting of funds will be consistent with normal operating procedures of a non-profit organization.

6.   Volunteers will not be paid for mileage or any services rendered considered within the scope of usual volunteer services.

EDUCATIONAL TRAINING

1.   The Director will provide educational services to the clinical professionals selected to be trained as Group Grief Therapy Leaders.

2.   A 60 hour course of study will be required for designation as a Group Grief Therapy Leader. 30 hours of course work plus 30 hours of clinical training in the group setting with homicide survivors will be required.

3.   Licensed mental health professionals from local mental health agencies will be awarded first priority for positions in training.

4.   A position as clinical trainee may be awarded to students who are pursuing a full-time course of study in the fields of thanatology, psychology, counseling, psychiatric nursing, or social work.

5.   The Director will provide training to three groups of volunteers per year. Homicide survivors who have completed a course of Group Grief Therapy and, in the opinion of the psychotherapist, are capable of providing services to other survivors will have the first priority in application to be trained as volunteers.

6.   Positions in the Volunteer Training Course will be opened to the victim advocates who, by position or title, work in the police departments, Sheriff's Office or other delivery systems for victims of crime.

7.   No more than 12 persons will be accepted for training classes in any one course of training.

8.   The course will provide 12 hours of volunteer training in a six week time period. Grief therapy training may open up old unresolved grief issues in the trainee's personal life. These demand attention and resolution prior to working with new survivors. The instructor must be prepared for this occurrence and be available to the trainee.

9.   Classes will not be scheduled in subsequent days. In order to effectively learn the affective, cognitive, and behavioral components of crisis intervention, time must be provided to the trainee for internalization, reflection and completion of assignments.

10. Materials will be provided to trainees. Books which will be available for check-out must be returned on schedule.

COMMUNITY EDUCATION

1.   Educational programs will be offered to the community on a contractual basis.

2.   Interviews on media networks: television, radio, or press coverage, will be directed to education of the public.

ADDITIONAL PROFESSIONAL EDUCATION

1.   Seminars, workshops, and conferences will be provided to other mental health professionals and victim advocates on a contractual basis.

2.   Those who reside or work in the state will be awarded first priority for educational services.

3.   The cost of materials and preparation for training will be expended from the budget of HSGP.

SHORT-TERM PLANNING

1. One course of Group Grief Therapy will be provided to ten homicide survivors in 1986, October - December.

2. Three groups will be offered in 1987. One from February to April, and two from September to November.

3. Six groups will be offered in 1988. These will be scheduled by HSGP to be provided every three months, i.e., January, April, July and October.

4. Twelve groups will be scheduled for 1989. One to begin each month of the year.

5. Two psychotherapists will be trained in 1986.

6. Six psychotherapists will be trained in 1987.

7. Twelve psychotherapists will be trained in 1988.

8. Each approved Grief Group Leader will select one clinical trainee as co-leader for each group offered.

9. Thirty-six volunteers or victim advocates will be provided homicide survivor crisis intervention training skills for each year of operation. (Twelve students will be provided training for each of three classes.)

LONG-RANGE PLANNING

1. Plans to teach and train psychotherapists and victim advocates will be extended to other state agencies throughout the development of this program.

2. Contact with NOVA, Parents of Murdered Children, Inc., National Victim Center, Inc., and MADD will be developed for national training efforts.

3. An educational film is under production and will be available for national training programs.

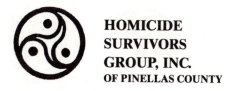

**HOMICIDE
SURVIVORS
GROUP, INC.**
OF PINELLAS COUNTY

DONATIONS

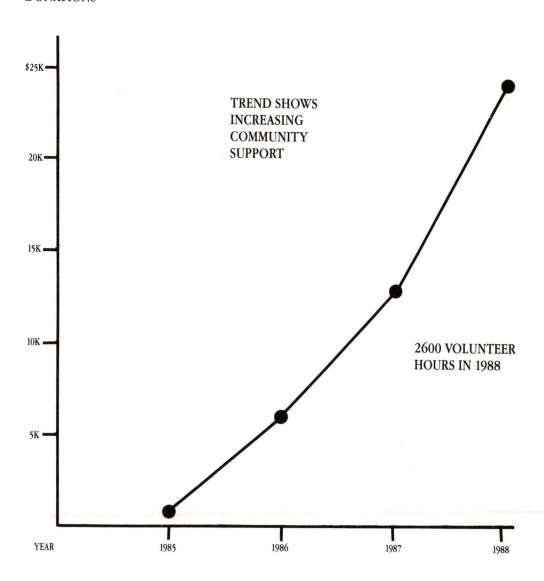

**HOMICIDE
SURVIVORS
GROUP, INC.**
OF PINELLAS COUNTY

CLIENTS

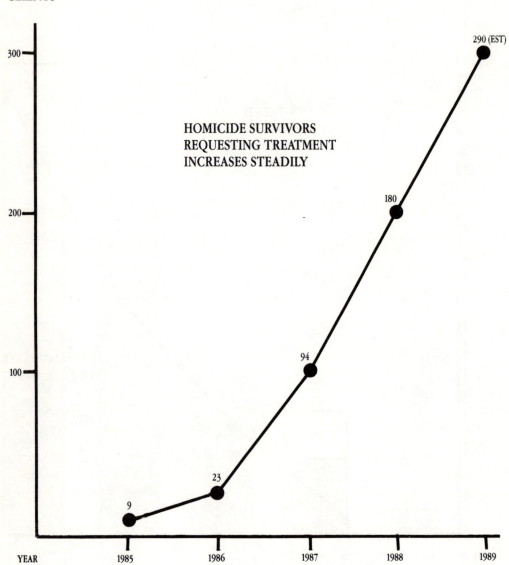

HOMICIDE SURVIVORS
REQUESTING TREATMENT
INCREASES STEADILY

290 (EST)

300

200

180

100

94

23

9

YEAR   1985   1986   1987   1988   1989

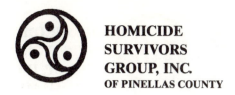

**HOMICIDE
SURVIVORS
GROUP, INC.**
OF PINELLAS COUNTY

FINANCES

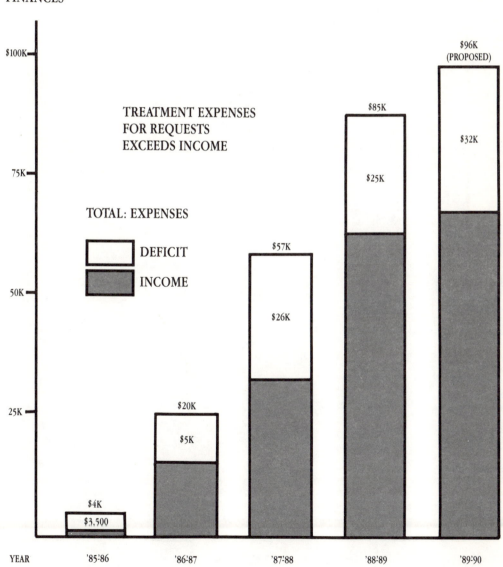

TREATMENT EXPENSES
FOR REQUESTS
EXCEEDS INCOME

TOTAL: EXPENSES

☐ DEFICIT
▓ INCOME

$100K

$96K
(PROPOSED)

$85K

$32K

$75K

$25K

$57K

$26K

50K

$20K

25K

$5K

$4K

$3,500

YEAR   '85-'86   '86-'87   '87-'88   '88-'89   '89-'90

REFERENCES

SUGGESTED READING FOR GROUP MEMBERS

Bolton, Iris with Mitchell, Curtis, *My Son. . . My Son. . .*, *A Guide to Healing After a Suicide in the Family,* Bolton Press, GA, 1984.

Burns, Maureen A. & Burns, Cara M, *Life and Death in Third Grade,* Empey Enterprises, MI, 1987.

Caine, Lynn, *Widow,* Bantam Books, NY, 1985.

Colgrove, Melba; Bloomfield, Harold H.; and McWilliams, Peter, *How To Survive The Loss Of A Love, 58 Things To Do When There Is Nothing To Be Done,* Bantam Books, NY, 1981.

Gordon, Audrey K. & Klass, Dennis, *They Need to Know, How to Teach Children about Death,* Prentice-Hall, Inc., NJ, 1979.

Gottman, John; Notarius, Cliff; Gonso, Jonni; and Markman, Howard, *A Couple's Guide to Communication,* Research Press Company, IL, 1976.

Grollman, Earl A., *Talking About Death, A Dialogue Between Parent And Child,* Beacon Press, Boston, 1976.

Hughes, Phyllis Rash, *Dying is Different,* Mech Mentor Educational Publishers, IL, 1978.

Jampolsky, Gerald G., *Love Is Letting Go Of Fear,* Bantam Books, NY, 1981.

Jensen, Amy Hillyard, *Healing Grief,* Medic Publishing Company, WA, 1980.

Johnson, Joy & Johnson, S.M., *Children Die Too, A book for parents who have experienced the death of a child,* Centering Corporation, NE, 1981.

Johnson, Joy & Marv, *Tell Me, Papa, A family book for children's questions about death and funerals,* Centering Corporation, NE, 1982.

Kicr, Ari, *Recovery from Depression, A Self-Help Strategy,* E.P. Dutton, NY, 1982.

Kollar, Nathan R., *Songs of Suffering,* Winston Press, MN, 1982.

Kushner, Harold, S., *When Bad Things Happen To Good People,* First Avon Printing, NY, 1983.

LeShan, Eda, *Learning To Say Good-by, When A Parent Dies,* MacMillan Publishing Company, Inc., NY, 1976.

Levy, Erin Linn, *Children Are Not Paper Dolls,* IL, 1982.

Lord, Janice Harris, *No Time For Goodbyes, Coping With Grief, Anger, and Injustice After A Tragic Death,* Pathfinder Publishing, CA, 1987.

Morgan, Ernest, *Dealing Creatively with Death, A Manual of Death Education and Simple Burial,* Celo Press, NC, 1988.

O'Conner, Nancy, *Letting Go With Love,* La Mariposa Press, 1984.

Parrish-Hara, Carol W., *A New Age Handbook for Death and Dying,* Divorss & Company, CA, 1982.

President's Child Safety Partnership, Final Report, Washington, D.C.,1987.

Schiff, Harriet Sarnoff, *The Bereaved Parent,* Peguin Books Ltd., England, 1984.

Scrivani, Mark T., *Love, Mark, A Series of Letters on Grief For Children* (And Those Who Used To Be), Hope For Bereaved, NY, 1988.

Stark, James H. & Goldstein, Howard W., *The Rights of Crime Victims,* Bantam Books, NY, 1985.

Staudacher, Carol, *Beyond Grief, A Guide for Recovering from the Death of a Loved One,* New Harbinger Publications, Inc., CA, 1987.

Stearns, Ann Kaiser, *Living Through Personal Crisis,* Ballantine Books, NY, 1984.

Stiles, Norman, *I'll Miss You, Mr. Hooper,* Random House/Children's Television Workshop, NY, 1984.

The Center for Attitudinal Healing, *There Is A Rainbow Behind Every Dark Cloud,* Celestial Arts, CA, 1979.

Varley, Susan, *Badger's Parting Gifts,* Andersen Press Ltd., London, 1984.

Westberg, Granger E., *Good Grief, A Constructive Approach to the Problem of Loss,* Fortress Press, PA, 1981.

REFERENCE NOTES

Chapter 1

1. Kubler-Ross, Elisabeth, *On Death And Dying,* MacMilliam Publishing Company, Inc., New York, 1969.

2. Miller, Katherine; Moore, Nancy; and Lexius, Charles, News and Views, "A Group for Families of Homicide Victims: An Evaluation," *Social Casework: The Journal of Contemporary Social Work,* Family Service America, September 1985.

3. *The Uniform Crime Reports,* Federal Bureau of Investigation, Washington, D.C., 1986.

4. Ibid.

5. Redmond, Lula M., case files of author.

6. National Organization for Victim Assistance (NOVA), 717 D Street NW, Washington, D.C. 20004.

7. Parents of Murdered Children (POMC), 1739 Bella Vista, Cincinnati, Ohio 45237.

8. National Victim Center (NVC), 307 West 7th Street, Suite 1001, Fort Worth, Texas 76102.

9. van der Kolk, Bessel A., *Psychological Trauma,* American Psychiatric Press, Inc., Washington, D.C., 1987, p. 162.

10. Horowitz, Mardi Jon, Stress Response Syndromes, 2nd edition, Aronson Press, New York, 1985.

11. van der Kolk, ibid., p. 162-167.

12. Osterweis, Marian; Killilea, Marie; and Greer, David, "Bereavement Intervention Programs" in *Bereavement: Reactions, Consequences and Care,* ed. by Marian Osterweis, Fredric Solomon, Morris Green, National Academy Press, Washington, D.C., 1984.

13. Yalom, Irvin D., *The Theory and Practice of Group Psychotherapy,* 2nd ed., Basic Books, Inc., New York 1975.

14. Worden, J. William, *Grief Counseling and Grief Therapy, A Handbook for the Mental Health Practitioner,* Springer Publishing Company, New York, 1982.

15. Rando, Therese A., *Grief, Dying, and Death: Clinical Interventions For Caregivers,* Research Press, Champaign, Illinois, 1984.

16. van der Kolk, ibid., 1987.

17. Kavanaugh, Robert, *Facing Death,* Penguin Books, Baltimore, Maryland, 1974.

18. Rando, ibid., p.9-13.

Chapter 2

1.   Shaw, George Bernard, quote from Nightingale Conant tapes, Chicago, Illinois, 1988.

2.   The Compassionate Friends, Inc. (TCF), P.O. Box 3696, Oak Brook, Illinois 60522.

3.   POMC, ibid.

4.   Mothers Against Drunk Driving (MADD), 669 Airport Freeway, Suite 310, Hurst, Texas 76053.

5.   *National Crime Survey,* U.S. Department of Justice, Bureau of Justice Statistics, Washington, D.C.

6.   *The Uniform Crime Reports,* Federal Bureau of Investigation, Washington, D.C.

7.   Pinellas County Victim's Rights Coalition, Inc., P.O. Box 304, Largo, FL 34292-0304.

8.   Florida Network of Victim/Witness Services, Inc., P.O. Box 2882, Gainesville, FL 32602.

9.   Association for Death Education and Counseling, Inc. (ADEC), 638 Prospect Avenue, Hartford, Connecticut 06105.

10. ADEC National Certification Review Board, 5 Bradford Road, Rochester, New York 14618.

11. NOVA, ibid.

12. NVC, ibid.

13. POMC, ibid.

14. MADD, ibid.

15. The Society for Traumatic Stress Studies, P.O. Box 1564, Lancaster, Pennsylvania 17603-1564.

16. League of Victim and Empathizers, Inc. (LOVE), 1930 Florida Avenue, Palm Harbor, Florida 34683.

17. National Victim's Resource Center, Office of Victims of Crime, 633 Indiana Avenue NW, Room 1352, Washington, D.C. 20531.

18. Mental Health Services of Upper Pinellas, Inc., 1437 South Belcher Rd., Clearwater, FL 34646.

Chapter 3

1. Bowlby, John, "The Making and Breaking of Affectional Bonds," *British Journal of Psychiatry,* 1977, p.201-210; 421-431.

2. Worden, ibid., p.8.

3. Lindemann, Eric, "Symptomatology and management of acute grief," American Journal of Psychiatry 101: (1944): 141- 148.

4. Caplan, Gerald, *Principles of Preventive Psychiatry,* Basic Books, New York, 1962.

5. Bowlby, John, *Attachment and Loss: Loss, Sadness, and Depression,* Vol.III, Basic Books, New York, 1980.

6. Engel, George, "Is Grief A Disease?," *Psychosomatic Medicine,* 1961, p. 18-22.

7. Paul, Norman, Death in the Family System, seminar presentation, 2nd International Conference on Grief and Bereavement, London, England, 1988.

8. Davidson, Glen W., Hospice Care For The Dying, *Dying Facing The Facts,* ed. H. Wass, Hemisphere Publishing, Washington, D.C., 1979, p. 174.

9. ibid.

10. ibid.

11. Worden, ibid., p. 20-28.

12. Lifton, Robert Jay, *The Broken Connection,* Simon & Schuster, New York, 1979, p. 147.

13. ibid., p. 148.

14. ibid., p. 151.

15. Bard, Morton, and Dawn Sangrey, *The Crime Victim's Book,* Citadel Press, New York, 1986, p. 45.

16.   Sanders, Catherine M., Paul A. Mauger, Paschal N. Strong, Jr., *A Manual For The Grief Experience Inventory (Research Edition),* Consulting Psychologists Press, Inc., Palo Alto, CA. 1979, 1985.

17.   Lord, Janice Harris, "Death Notification Procedure," MADDVOCATE, publication by Mothers Against Drunk Driving, 1988.

18.   Watzlawick, Paul, *Ultra-Solutions or How To Fail Most Successfully,* W.W. Norton, New York, 1988, p. 69.

19.   Amick-McMullan, Angelynne, Kilpatrick, Dean G., Veronen, Lois J., Smith, Susan, "Family Survivors of Homicide Victims: Theoretical Perspectives and an Exploratory Study," *Journal of Traumatic Stress,* Vol.2: 1:21-33: 1989.

20.   Lindemann, ibid.

21.   Krystal, H., *Massive Psychic Trauma,* International Universities Press, New York, 1968.

22.   Lifton, ibid.

23.   van der Kolk, Bessel A., *Psychological Trauma,* American Psychiatric Press, Washington, D.C., 1987, p. 153.

24.   Erickson, K.T., *Everything In Its Path: Destruction of Community in the Buffalo Creek Flood,* Simon & Schuster, NY, 1976.

Chapter 4

1.   Neiderbach, Shelley, "Do No Harm," Networks, Vol. 3:2, National Victim Center, June 1988.

2.   Rando, ibid., 1984.

3.   Carter, Elizabeth A., Monica McGoldrick, eds. *The Family Life Cycle,* Gardner Press, NY, 1980, p. 3-20.

4.   *Diagnostic and Statistical Manual of Mental Disorders, Third Edition, Revised 1987,* American Psychiatric Association, Washington, D.C.

5.   NOVA, *Crisis Response Team Training Manual,* Washington, D.C., 1987.

6.   Worden, ibid.

7.   McGoldrick, Monica, Randy Gerson, *Genograms in Family Assessment,* W.W. Norton & Company, NY, 1985.

8. Sanders, et.al. ibid., 1979.

9. Lifton, ibid.

Chapter 5

1. "Grief Symptomatology," outline of normal bereavement symptoms, adapted from Worden, J.W., *Grief Counseling and Grief Therapy,* 1982.

2. Harper, Jeanne, presentation at Tenth Annual Conference, Association For Death Education and Counseling, Inc., 1987, Atlanta, GA.

3. Redmond, Lula M., handout developed for clients in therapy, 1979.

4. Bowen, M., "Family Reaction To Death," ed. P. Guerin, *Family Therapy, Theory and Practice,* 1976, p. 335-348.

5. Lattanzi, M., National Hospice Organization conference presentation, St. Louis, Missouri, 1984.

6. Grollman, Earl A., *What Helped Me When My Loved One Died,* Beacon Press, Boston, Massachusetts, 1981.

7. Conner, P., "Guided Journal Work As An Aid To Resolving Grief," paper presented at Association For Death Education and Counseling Conference, London, Canada, 1987.

8. Knapp, Ronald J., "The Family and Bereavement" Course of Adjustment: Parental Response to the Murder of a Child, *Beyond Endurance, When A Child Dies,* Schocken Books, New York, 1986, p. 124-153.

9. Jackson, Edgar N., "Bereavement and Grief," p. 256-281; Davidson, Glen W., "Mourning Process Not Understood," p. 173-180, in Wass, Hannelore, ed, *Dying, Facing The Facts,* Hemisphere Publishing Corporation, New York, 1979.

10. Rando, Therese A., *Grief, Dying, and Death; Clinical Interventions for Caregivers,* Research Press, Champaign Illinois, 1984, p. 76-79.

11. ibid., p. 43-57.

12. Sanders, Catherine, "Bereavement Typologies and Implications for Therapy," Forum Newsletter, Association for Death Education and Counseling, Inc., Vol.7, No. 1, January, 1984.

13. Bowlby, John, and Colin Murray Parkes, "Separation and Loss Within The Family,"

E.J. Anthony, C. Koupernik, ed. *The Child in His Family,* Wiley Company, New York 1970.

14.   Worden, J. William, *Grief Counseling and Grief Therapy,* Springer Publishing Company, New York, 1982, p. 11-17.

15.   "Survivors of Homicide Victims," Network Information Bulletin, NOVA, Vol. 2., No. 3, October 1985.

16.   Lifton, Robert J., "The Sense of Immortality: On Death and the Continuity of Life," in Feifel, H., ed. *New Meanings of Death,* McGraw-Hill, New York, 1977, p. 274-289.

17.   ibid., 1977, p. 274-289.

18.   Rando, Therese A., "Sudden Versus Anticipated Death," *Grieving: How to Go on Living When Someone You Love Dies,* Lexinton Books, Lexington, Massachusetts, 1988, p. 89-106.

19.   Fulton, Robert, phamphlet, "Understanding the Experience of Grief," Center for Death Education and Research, Univ. of Minn., Minneapolis, Minnesota, 1984.

20.   van der Kolk, Bessel A., ed., *Post-Traumatic Stress Disorder: Psychological and Biological Sequelae,* American Psychiatric Press, Inc., Washington, D.C., 1984.

21.   *Diagnostic and Statistical Manual of Mental Disorders, Third Edition,* Revised, American Psychiatric Association, Washington, D.C., 1987.

22.   Bard, Morton, and Dawn Sangrey, "Why Me? The Search for a Reason," *The Crime Victim's Book,* Citadel Press, New Jersey, 1986, p. 53-75.

23.   Lifton, ibid., 1979: p. 147-178.

24.   Hankins, Gary, *Prescription for Anger, Coping With Angry Feelings and Angry People,* Princess Publishing, Beaverton, Oregon, 1988.

25.   Lifton, ibid., 1979, p. 147.

26.   ibid., p. 177-178.

27.   Hankins, ibid.

28.   Bard, Morton, and Dawn Sangrey, "The Mark: Feelings of Guilt and Shame," *The Crime Victim's Book,* Citadel Press, New Jersey, 1986, p. 76-102.

29. Worden, J. William, *Grief Counseling and Grief Therapy,* Springer Publishing, New York, 1982, p. 13.

Chapter 6

1. Worden, ibid., p.11-12; 210.

2. Osmont, Kelly, and Marilyn McFarlane, "What Can I Say?," *Parting Is Not Goodbye,* Nobility Press, Portland, Oregon, 1986.

3. Ramsay, Ronald, W. and Noorbergen, Rene, *Living With Loss: A Dramatic New Breakthrough in Grief Therapy,* William Morrow and Company, New York, 1981.

4. Bowen, Murray, *Family Therapy: Theory and Practice,* "Family Reaction to Death," Philip J. Guerin, Jr., ed. Gardner Press, Inc., New York, 1976, p. 335-348.

5. Bowen, ibid., p. 335-336.

6. Ramsay, ibid.

7. Bowen, ibid., p. 344-348.

8. Rando, Therese A., "Funerals and Funerary Rituals," *Grief, Dying, and Death: Clinical Interventions for Caregivers,* Research Press, Champaign, Illinois, 1984, p. 173-197.

9. Stephenson, John S., "Ceremonies of Death: The Funeral," *Death, Grief, and Mourning,* The Free Press, New York, p. 198-234.

10. Worden, ibid., p.14.

11. Morgan, Ernest, "Sample Death Ceremonies," *A Manual of Death Education and Simple Burial,* Celo Press, North Carolina, 1984, p. 122-142.

12. Volkan, Vamik D., "Introduction; The Evolution of Research Into Complicated Mourning" , p. 1-154; "Re-Grief Therapy," p. 201-233 ; *Linking Objects and Linking Phenomena: A Study of the Forms, Symptoms, Metapsychology, and Therapy of Complicated Mourning,* International Universities Press, Inc., New York, 1981.

13. Pine, Vanderlyn R., A. Kutscher, D. Peretz, R.Slater, R. DeBellis, R. Volk, & D. Cherico, eds. *Acute Grief and the Funeral,* Charles C. Thomas, Springfield, Illinois, 1976.

14. Lifton, Robert Jay, *The Broken Connection, On Death and the Continuity of Life,* Simon & Schuster, New York, 1979, p. 177.

15. Volkan, ibid.

16. Osterweis, et. al., ibid.

17. Rando, Therese A., *Parental Loss Of A Child,* Research Press, Champaign, Illinois, 1986, p. 5-119; 341-413.

18. Worden, William J., *Grief Counseling and Grief Therapy, A Handbook for the Mental Health Practitioner,* Springer Publishing Company, New York, 1982, p. 11-16.

19. Sanders, Catherine M., Paul A. Mauger, Paschal N. Strong, Jr., *A Manual For The Grief Experience Inventory,* Consulting Psychologists Press, 577 College Avenue, Palo Alto, California, 1979, 1985.

20. Worden, ibid., p. 11-16.

21. Davidson, Glen W., "Mourning Process Not Understood," *Dying: Facing The Facts,* ed. Hannelore Wass, Hemisphere Publishing Corporation, New York, 1979, p. 178.

22. Sanders, ibid., 1979, p. 5.

BIBLIOGRAPHY

Aguilera, Donna C. & Messick, Janice M., *Crisis Intervention,* Theory and Methodology, The C.V. Mosby Co., St. Louis, 1986.

Alberti, Robert E. & Emmons, Michael L., *Your Perfect Right, A Guide to Assertive Behavior,* Impact Publishers, California, 1978.

American Association of Suicidology, Central Office, 2459 South Ash, Denver, Colorado 80222.

Amick-McMullan, A., Kilpatrick, D., Veronen, L., Smith, S., "Family Survivors of Homicide Victims: Theoretical Perspectives and an Exploratory Study," *Journal of Traumatic Stress,* Vol.2:1,1989.

An American Civil Liberties Union Handbook, *The Rights of Crime Victims,* 1983.

Association for Death Education and Counseling (ADEC), 638 Prospect Avenue, Hartford, Connecticut 06105.

Attorney General's Task Force on Family Violence, Final Report, Washington, D.C., September 1984.

Bard, Morton & Sangrey, Dawn, *The Crime Victim's Book,* Citadel Press, New Jersey, 1986.

Bates, Meg, "Network Establishes Statewide Crisis Response Team," The Florida Network of Victim Witness Services, Inc., Winter 1988.

Becker, Ernest, *The Denial of Death,* The Free Press, New York, 1973.

Bowen, Murray, "Family, Reaction to Death," *Family Therapy, Theory and Practice,* ed. Philip J. Guerin, Gardner Press, Inc., New York, 1976.

Bowlby, John, *Attachment and Loss,* Volume I, Attachment, Basic Books, Inc., New York, 1969.

Bowlby, John, *Attachment and Loss,* Volume II, Separation, Anxiety and Anger, Basic Books, Inc., New York, 1973.

Bowlby, John, *Attachment and Loss,* Volume III, Loss, Sadness and Depression, Basic Books, Inc., New York, 1980.

Feifel, Herman, *New Meanings of Death,* McGraw-Hill Book Co., New York, 1977.

Figley, Charles R. & McCubbin, Hamilton I., *Stress and the Family, Volume II: Coping With Catastrophe,* Brunner/Mazel, Inc., New York, 1983.

Figley, Charles R., *Trauma and Its Wake, Volume II: Traumatic Stress Theory, Research, and Intervention,* Brunner/Mazel, Inc., New York, 1986.

Gartner, Alan & Riessman, Frank, *Self-Help In The Human Services,* Jossey-Bass, Inc., California, 1977.

Gill, Derek, *Quest, The Life of Elisabeth Kubler-Ross,* Harper & Row, New York, 1980.

Goldenberg, Herbert & Goldenberg, Irene, "Homicide and The Family," *The Human Side of Homicide,* Danto, Bruce L.; Bruhns, John; and Kutscher, Austin H., eds., Columbia University Press, New York, 1982.

Greenberg, Herbert M., *Coping With Job Stress, A Guide For Employers & Employees,* Prentice Hall, Inc., New Jersey, 1980.

Grollman, Earl A., *Concerning Death, A Practical Guide for the Living,* Beacon Press, Boston, Massachusetts, 1974.

Guerin, Philip J., *Family Therapy, Theory and Practice,* Gardner Press, Inc., New York, 1976.

Hankins, Gary, *Prescription for Anger, Coping with Angry Feelings and Angry People,* Princess Publishing, Oregon, 1988.

Kastenbaum, Robert, & Aisenberg, R., *The Psychology of Death,* Springer Publishing Co., New York, 1972.

Kerr, Micheal E. & Bowen, Murray, *Family Evaluation, An Approach Based on Bowen Theory,* W.W. Norton & Co., New York, 1988.

Knapp, Ronald J., *Beyond Endurance, When a Child Dies,* Schocken Books, New York, 1986.

Liff, Zanvel A., *The Leader in the Group,* Jason Aronson, Inc., New York, 1975.

Lifton, Robert J., *The Broken Connection, On Death and the Continuity of Life,* Simon and Schuster, New York, 1979.

Lindemann, Eric, "Symptomatology and Management of Acute Grief," *American Journal of Psychiatry,* 1944, 101;141-148.

Lynch, James J., *The Broken Heart,* Basic Books, New York, 1977.

McGoldrick, Monica & Gerson, Randy, *Genograms in Family Assessment,* W.W. Norton & Co., New York, 1985.

Members Task Force, *Attorney General's Task Force on Family Violence,* Final Report, September 1984.

Merck, Sharp, and Dohme, Health Information Services, West Point, Pennsylvania 19486.

Mothers Against Drunk Driving (MADD), 669 Airport Freeway, Suite 310, Hurst, Texas 76053.

National Institute of Mental Health, Mental Health Emergencies Section, 5600 Fishers Lane, Rockville, Maryland 20852.

National Institute of Justice, *NIJ Reports,* ''Experiments Help Shape New Policies,'' U.S. Department of Justice, September/October 1988.

National Victim's Resource Center, Office of Victims of Crime, 633 Indiana Avenue NW, Room 1352, Washington, D.C. 20531.

Neiderbach, Shelley, *Invisible Wounds: Crime Victims Speak,* The Haworth Press, New York, 1986.

Osmont, Kelly & McFarlane, Marilyn, *What Can I Say?, How to help someone who is Grieving: A Guide,* Nobility Press, Oregon 1988.

Osterweis, Marian; Solomon, Fredric; and Green, Morris, *Bereavement, Reactions, Consequences, and Care,* National Academy Press, Washington, D.C., 1984.

Parkes, Colin Murray, et al, ''Broken Heart: A Statistical Study of Increased Mortality Among Widower's,'' *British Medical Journal* 1, 1969.

Pittman, Frank S., *Turning Points, Treating Families in Transition and Crisis,* W.W. Norton & Co., New York, 1987.

Ramsay, Ronald W.; Noorbergen, Rene, *Living With Loss, A Dramatic New Breakthrough in Grief Therapy,* William Morrow and Company, New York, 1981.

Rando, Therese A., *Grief, Dying, and Death, Clinical Interventions for Caregivers,* Research Press Co, Illinois, 1984.

Rando, Therese A., *Loss and Anticipatory Grief,* Lexington Books, Massachusetts, 1986.

Rando, Therese A., *Grieving, How to Go on Living When Someone You Love Dies,* Lexington Books, Massachusetts, 1988.

Raphael, Beverly, *The Anatomy of Bereavement,* Basic Books, New York, 1983.

Rosen, Helen, *Unspoken Grief, Coping with Childhood Sibling Loss,* Lexington Books, Massachusetts, 1987.

Rubin, Theodore Isaac, *The Angry Book,* Collier Books, New York, 1969.

Sanders, Catherine M., Mauger, Paul A., Strong, Paschal N., Jr. *A Manual For The Grief Experience Inventory,* Consulting Psychologists Press, Inc., Palo Alto, California, 1979; 1985.

Schoenberg, Bernard; Carr, Arthur C.; Peretz, David; and Kuscher, Austin H., *Loss and Grief, Psychological Management in Medical Practice,* Columbia University Press, New York, 1970.

Shneidman, Edwin S., *Death: Current Perspectives,* Mayfield Publishing Co., California, 1980.

Solomon, Marion F., *Narcissism and Intimacy, Love and Marriage in an Age of Confusion,* W.W. Norton & Co., New York, 1989.

Stein, John H., "Voca Revisited, Reauthorized, and Revitalized, 'Underserved Populations of Victims of Violent Crime' To Get Aid," NOVA Newsletter, Volume 12, Number 10, October 1988.

Stephenson, John S., *Death, Grief, and Mourning, Individual and Social Realities,* The Free Press, New York, 1985.

Stillman, Frances A., "Line-of-Duty Deaths: Survivor and Departmental Responses," *Research in Brief,* National Institute of Justice, January 1987.

Suicide Information Center, 6377 Lake Apopka Place, San Diego, California 92119.

Suicide Prevention Center, Inc., 184 Salem Avenue, Dayton, Ohio 45406.

Tsui, Philip & Schultz, Gail L., "Ethnic Factors In Group Process: Cultural Dynamics in Multi-Ethnic Therapy Groups, *American Journal Orthopsychiatry* 58: January 1988.

van der Kolk, Bessel A., *Post-Traumatic Stress Disorder: Psychological and Biological Sequelae,* American Psychiatric Press, Inc., Washington, D.C., 1984.

van der Kolk, Bessel A., *Psychological Trauma,* American Psychiatric Press, Inc., Washington, D.C., 1987.

Volkan, Vamik D., *Linking Objects And Linking Phenomena, A Study of the Forms, Symptoms, Metapsychology, and Therapy of Complicated Mourning,* International Universities Press, New York, 1981.

Washington Legal Foundation, *Court Watch Manual: A Citizen's Guide to Judicial Accountability,* Washington Legal Foundation, Washington, D.C., 1982.

Wass, Hannelore, *Dying, Facing the Facts,* Hemisphere Publishing Corporation, Washington & New York, 1979.

Wass, Hannelore, & Corr, Charles A., *Helping Children Cope with Death, Guidelines and Resources,* Hemisphere Publishing Corporation, Washington & New York, 1982.

Watzlawick, Paul, *Ultra-Solutions or How to Fail Most Successfully,* W.W. Norton & Co., New York, 1988.

Wilks, John, "Murder in Mind," Psychology Today, June 1987.

Williams, Tom, *Post-Traumatic Stress Disorders: A Handbook for Clinicians,* Disabled American Veterans, Ohio, 1987.

Worden, J. William, *Grief Counseling and Grief Therapy, A Handbook for the Mental Health Practitioner,* Springer Publishing Co., New York, 1982.

Yalom, Irvin D., *The Theory And Practice Of Group Psychotherapy,* Second Edition, Basic Books, Inc., New York, 1975.

Zisook, Sidney, *Biopsychosocial Aspects of Bereavement,* American Psychiatric Press, Inc., Washington, D.C., 1987.

INDEX

ADEC HISTORY

The Association for Death Education and Counseling **ADEC** was created in 1976 as FORUM for Death Education and Counseling. **ADEC** is the oldest interdisciplinary organization in the field of death, dying and bereavement. The membership is made up of educators, nurses, physicians, hospital and hospice personnel, mental health professionals, clergy, funeral directors, social workers, philosophers, physical and recreation therapists, health and well-being specialists and volunteers.

ADEC works to promote and share research, theories and practice in death, dying and bereavement so that professionals and lay persons may be better able to meet the needs of those they work with in death education and counseling.

ADEC GOALS

Through elected representatives from the membership and over a dozen standing committees, **ADEC** is working on its unique way to:

- Promote responsible and effective education and counseling.
- Upgrade the quality of death education in educational institutions at all levels, in hospitals, in residential care facilities, in churches, in community and non-profit organizations, and in government facilities and operations.
- Improve the quality of counseling in the areas of death, dying and bereavement.

MEMBERSHIP BENEFITS

- **FORUM,** a professional newsletter published eight times per year, featuring original articles, book and audio-visual reviews, and current items of interest.
- **Annual International Conference** to focus on up-to-date information and afford colleagual sharing among members in a warm, supportive and stimulating atmosphere.
- Opportunities to **PRESENT ASPECTS OF YOUR WORK** to other members at regional and national meetings.
- Low cost **CONFERENCE PROCEEDINGS** which contain an outstanding selection of presentations and papers by **ADEC** members and invited keynote speakers.
- Participation in developing and promoting **CODES OF ETHICS AND STANDARDS OF TRAINING** for death educators and counselors.
- An **ANNUAL MEMBERSHIP DIRECTORY.**
- An **INTERNATIONAL NETWORK OF RESOURCE PERSONS** for referral.
- **DISCOUNT RATES** for major journals in the field.
- **REGIONAL CHAPTER** eligibility for local participation.
- **BOOK SERVICE** providing discounts and ready access to a variety of materials in the field.
- **ADVANCE NOTICE DISCOUNTS** on National and Regional programs sponsored by **ADEC** to enable members to augment their teaching and caregiving skills.
- Optional **CERTIFICATION** as a Death Educator and/or Grief Counselor.

APPLICATION FOR MEMBERSHIP

Individual Membership . . . . $50 (U.S.) _____

Institutional Membership . . . . . $100 (U.S.)_____
(Institution has the organization's name/address listed in the directory. They can also specify two members of the organization who are accorded full membership privileges.)

Student Membership . . . . $35 (U.S.)_____
(Full-time graduate or undergraduate students. Please submit documentation.)

Older Citizen Membership . . . . . $35 (U.S.)_____
(62 plus)

Make check or money order payable to:

**ASSOCIATION FOR DEATH
EDUCATION AND COUNSELING
638 Prospect Avenue
Hartford, CT 06105**

ADEC is a tax-exempt non-profit organization.

Name _____

Organization (optional) _____

    Home ☐   Work ☐

Address _____

City_____ State_____ Zip_____

Phone: Home_____ Work_____

PLEASE CIRCLE APPROPRIATE OCCUPATION(S):

A - Nurse	F - Clergy/Religious
B - Social Worker	G - Writer/Editor
C - Higher Education	H - Funeral Director
D - Elem./Sec. Educ.	I - Hospice
E - Student	J - Counselor/Psychologist

K - Other (physicians, program directors, retired, etc.)

ORDER FORM

BOOKS:

To order, simply complete this self-contained order form and mail it with your check or money order today.

Price: $19.95 (add $2.60 per copy postage and handling)

☐ Please send me_____ copies of *Surviving: When Someone You Love Was Murdered.*

Enclosed is check or money order for $_____ . Please make payable to:

Psychological Consultation and Education Services, Inc.
P.O. Box 6111
Clearwater, Florida 34618-6111

NAME _____

ORGANIZATION_____

ADDRESS_____ SUITE #_____

CITY_____ STATE_____ ZIP_____

NEWSLETTERS:

☐ Please send me the Quarterly Newsletter, *Changing Lives* @ $15.00 per year.

T-SHIRTS and BUMPER STICKERS:

☐ Please send me "Someone I Love Was Murdered" T-Shirt @ $6.00 each.

SPECIFY: ☐ MEDIUM ☐ LARGE ☐ X-LARGE

☐ Please send me "Someone I Love Was Murdered" Bumper Sticker @ $2.00.

Enclosed is check or money order for $_____ . Please make payable to:

Homicide Survivors Group, Inc.
P.O. Box 6201
Clearwater, Florida 34618-6201

NAME _____

ORGANIZATION_____

ADDRESS_____ SUITE #_____

CITY_____ STATE_____ ZIP_____

ALLOW FOUR TO SIX WEEKS FOR DELIVERY